Tasty Foods Along Minnesota Highways

D1714558

TASTY FOODS
ALONG
MINNESOTA
HIGHWAYS

Patricia A. Overson

NORTH STAR PRESS OF ST. CLOUD, INC.
St. Cloud, Minnesota

Book cover design by Jon Flor at Dave's Great Ad Shop
Bloomington, MN
www.davesgreatadshop.com

Copyright © 2010 Patricia A. Overson
pattyotrivia@gmail.com
www.pattyotrivia.com

ISBN: 0-87839-379-X
ISBN-13: 978-0-87839-379-4

First Edition, August 1, 2010

Printed in the United States of America

Published by
North Star Press of St. Cloud, Inc.
P.O. Box 451
St. Cloud, Minnesota 56302

www.northstarpress.com

US/MN HIGHWAY 61

Made famous by Minnesota native Bob Dylan's album *Highway 61 Revisited,* U.S. Highway 61 offers breathtaking views of lakes, forests, bluffs, rivers, as well having access to some of Minnesota's most intriguing cities and towns.

Highway 61 runs from the Canadian border near Grand Portage all the way down to New Orleans (sometimes merging with other roads), much of it as part of the "Great River Road" following the Mississippi. The highway is part of the Lake Superior Circle Tour that runs through Minnesota, Ontario, Michigan, and Wisconsin.

On the northern end of the highway, running along Lake Superior, nature lovers enjoy wildlife such as hawks and deer. They can see cliffs, bluffs, rivers, and waterfalls. Quaint shops, art galleries, great food, and places to stay are tucked along Highway 61 as it passes through the North Shore towns.

On Highway 61's southern end in Minnesota, barges and boats ply the Mississippi and eagles circle overhead. The highway passes through Hastings, a small town that has retained its character even though it's close to St. Paul; the Prairie Island Indian Reservation, which houses both a wildlife refuge as well as a casino; Red Wing, home of Red Wing Boots and Red Wing Pottery; the Lake Pepin area

1

(a favorite getaway from the Twin Cities); and Winona, home to Winona State University and St. Mary's University.

Reference:

Barnard, R. Kent; 651-234-7504, Minnesota Department of Transportation.

The Great Minnesota Touring Book, Thomas Huhti. Trails Books, 2004.

Minnesota Department of Natural Resources www.dnr .state.mn.us.

RYDEN'S CAFE

9301 Ryden Rd, Hwy 61 Grand Portage MN, 55605
Ryden's Café is on Highway 61, the last stop before the border.
www.rydensstore.com

Most Popular Foods: Garbage Omlette, Fresh local herring, and Border Burger. The **Garbage Omlette** consists of, ham, bacon, sausage, onion, mushrooms, tomatoes and cheese, served with a side of homemade hashbrowns and toast. The **Herring** is served at breakfast, at lunch in a herring burger or as a dinner entree. They have their own light breading recipe. The **Border Burger** is a half-pound burger with bacon, cheese, lettuce, tomatoes and mayo . . . delish! They serve breakfast all day long and have several local specials—steak bites, chicken-fried steak, and biscuits and gravy.

Ryden's Cafe History: Ryden's is a family-owned business established in 1947. The third generation are waitresses and the fourth can be seen doing dishes. They relocated in 1963 when the highway moved to its present location thanks to the sound vision of Ed Ryden (grandfather to current owner). Ryden's Café is seasonal, open May to October.

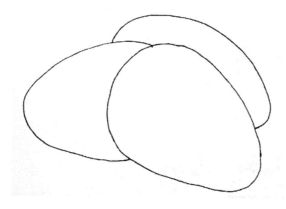

CHICAGO BAY MARKETPLACE BAKERY, DELI AND STORE

4971 East Highway 61 Hovland, MN 55606
(218) 475-2253
They are located on Highway 61 in Hovland.

Most Popular Foods: Homemade **Cinnamon Rolls**, homemade pizzas, and **Deli Sandwiches** on homemade bread. They're made from scratch cinnamon rolls can't be beat, and bring back memories of Grandma's baking. Their **Pizzas** are made on their homemade crust: white, fresh ground wheat, or multi-grain. **Deli Sandwiches** range from all veggie to high-quality roast beef, turkey, or ham. Sandwiches are served with parmesan and garlic or plain chips. They use high-quality light canola mayonnaise and organic mustard on homemade fresh ground whole grain breads with delicious, fresh lettuce, and tomatoes.

Chicago Bay Marketplace History: They opened the store in 2008 because the community surrounding Hovland wanted a store. As a local gathering place, they are a small community store working to serve the needs of their residents and guests. While dining, guests may hear the sound of the bread mixer and grain grinder in the kitchen,

making delicious, homemade food, the breads offered on the sandwiches and the wheat and rye flours used to make them. This gives their breads their supurb flavors and preserving the natural vitamins in the grain to a much greater degree than when pre-ground flours are used. Their deli meats and cheeses are high quality and reasonably priced, and they have many organic and natural selections, in addition to conventional foods.

Chicago Bay Marketplace is a sustainability oriented business, that believes in minimizing waste and maximizing quality. Their baked goods are the freshest in the area, and their doughs are from scratch. Selections of fresh breads and sweet treats are made daily. Varieties vary according to the needs of the deli, for use in their sandwiches, pizzas and special orders. They use natural, high quality ingredients in all of their recipes.

Chicago Bay was the name of Hovland until approximately 1900. The name was first used because so many folks from Chicago came across Lake Superior by boat in the summer to enjoy the cooler weather by the lake.

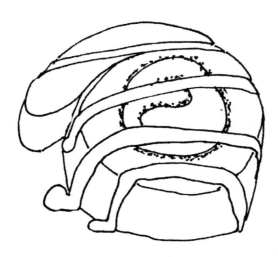

THE CROOKED SPOON CAFE

17 W Wisconsin Street Grand Marais, MN 55604
www. crookedspooncafe.com
1 block off highway 61. Turn right at the Intersection of Hwy 61 and
Broadway and another right at Wisconsin Street.

Most Popular Foods: Crab Cakes, Kobe Burger, Crooked BLT, French Onion Soup, Steaks, Fresh Fish, Sea Scallops, Duck Breast, Pastas and **Vegetarian Dishes**. Their Maryland **blue crab cakes** with firecracker jicama slaw and cilantro oil are the best.

Crooked Spoon Cafe History: Nathan and Sara Hingos opened the Crooked Spoon Cafe in August of 2006. It was something they had dreamed of doing for many years, and with a lot of help from family and friends the old "Jackson's Cafe" was transformed into a new and updated space. Since opening, Nathan has created new menus seasonally. He is always looking for new and inventive ways to take traditional fare down the "crooked" path!

CASCADE RESTAURANT

3719 West Highway 61, Lutsen MN 55612
www.cascadelodgemn.com/dining/
The restaurant is on Highway 61 overlooking Lake Superior.

Most Popular Food: Walleye pike, any fresh fish in season. Lightly breaded walleye fillet deep-fried until golden brown and served with tartar sauce, lemon, vegetables, and choice of potato. May be ordered broiled.

Cascade Restaurant History: This has been a North Shore favorite for over sixty years. Originally operated as a coffee shop/gas station, it became a seasonal restaurant in the 1950s and opened part time for winter business in 1970. It has been owned and operated by the O'Phelan family since 2004 and has been opened every day of the year except Christmas since then. They have worked tirelessly to provide handcrafted meals of the highest quality at an affordable price. Their menu is rich with choices including vegetarian items, and they also offer a full line of beverages including liquor options. They practice green policies and make every attempt at providing healthy choices to their guests.

PAPA CHARLIE'S

467 Ski Hill Road, Lutsen, MN 55612
www.lutsen.com   218-663-7800
Papa Charlie's is 2 miles off Highway 61.

Most Popular Food: Walleye Ruben Sandwich, a crisp, beer-battered walleye filet served between two slices of toasted marble rye with Swiss cheese, cole slaw, and thousand island dressing.

Papa Charlie's History: Located at the base of Lutsen Mountains Ski and Summer Resort, the Midwest's largest ski area, Papa Charlie's has both a restaurant and a tavern, as well as an arcade, billiards, ping-pong, live music, poker tournaments, and more. During ski season, folks can enjoy free après ski entertainment while they dine, enjoy a cocktail or play in the arcade—usually an acoustic performance by a local or regional artist or band. Every Friday features Comedy Night with a nationally touring comedian (free), followed by a late night band. Saturday nights bring more live music by regional or national bands (some of the most notable include Richard Thompson, Little Feat, Hot Tuna, Trampled by Turtles, Wookiefoot, Cloud Cult, Donna the Buffalo, The BoDeans, The Radiators, and more). Papa Charlie's is the "most happenin'" restaurant/night club on the North Shore!

In the spring, summer and fall, Papa Charlie's is a place to enjoy a more relaxed version of the atmosphere. Although Papa Charlie's does not have the entertainment during these months, guests enjoy casual dining—indoors or outside on the deck overlooking Moose Mountain and the Poplar River Valley. Kids of all ages love the arcade, ping pong table, and billiards. Papa Charlie's is a popular spot for weddings, rehearsal dinners, and other celebrations and functions.

BLUEFIN GRILLE

7192 W Hwy 61, Tofte, MN 55615
www.bluefinbay.com
Right on Hwy 61

Most popular items: Pan-Roasted Duck Breast, a marinated duck breast served with homemade cranberry chutney and béarnaise sauce. From home-style fair to refined dining, they specialize in delicious and reasonably priced cuisine. Other favorite specialties include **Hickory-Smoked Baby Back Ribs, Smoked Lake Superior Fish,** and **Coquilles St. Jacques** (jumbo sea scallops sautéed with shallots, garlic, wild mushrooms and finished with a champagne-cream reduction or 10 oz. hand-cut **filet mignon** flame-broiled and served with their signature Guinness and green peppercorn cream).

Bluefin Grille History: Opened in 1984, the same year the first townhomes of Bluefin Bay were finished. The original historical building was built in the 1940s, went through a few ownerships and remodelings, and in 1984 was reconstructed and turned into the Bluefin restaurant and bar. In 2005 the restaurant was remodeled and named Bluefin Grille.

The Bluefin Grille, located on the waterfront at Bluefin Bay, offers dining closer to Lake Superior than any other restaurant on the North Shore.

Bluefin Grille partners with well-known Midwest chefs and wine companies in May and November, for a well-known two-day Food and Wine Lovers Weekend. Guests can experience the culinary creations and perfect wine pairings.

COHO CAFE AND BAKERY

7126 W Hwy 61, Tofte, MN 55615
www.bluefinbay.com
Right on Hwy. 61.

Most Popular Food: Call of the Wild Pizza (homemade pizza crust, homemade tomato basil sauce, locally produced wild rice sausage, portabella, shiitake and button mushrooms piled with parmesan, romano, mozzarella, and provolone cheeses) and the **Primavera Pizza** (a vegetarian, homemade crust pizza, with basil pesto, marinated roma tomatoes, sautéed spinach, artichoke hearts, kalamata olives, button mushrooms, red onion, and browned parmesan, romano, mozzarella and provolone cheeses).

Coho Café and Bakery History: Opened in 1995 after the second part of Bluefin Bay in Tofte Cove was built, the Coho joined other restaurants on Bluefin Bay that served varied menus, so the Coho Café had to have a more specialized kitchen. The owners thought about light Italian menu with dishes made from scratch. Today Coho café is a casual, yet chic North Shore bistro. It serves specialty soups, sandwiches, and salads, its award-winning gourmet pizzas and pastas. Pastries, breads, scones, croissants, tortes, pies, and cakes are baked fresh daily.

JIMMY'S PIZZA & ICE CREAM SHOPPE

96 Outer Drive, Silver Bay, MN 55614
www.jimmyspizza.com
Seven-tenths of a mile off Highway 61.

Most Popular Foods: Jimmy's Deluxe Pizza, that has pepperoni, Italian sausage, onions, mushrooms, and green peppers. Also very popular is an item called a **Piega** (pie-egg-uh) — on the light side because when it comes out of the oven, it is stuffed with lettuce, tomato, veggies, and dressing.

Jimmy's Pizza & Ice Cream Shoppe History: This franchise, going for more than twenty years, is based out of Willmar, Minnesota. The Silver Bay location opened in 2005. They bought an existing restaurant that had just closed and kept some of the old equipment, but brought in a stone deck oven to cook their pizzas. They offer not only pizza, but soft serve ice cream.

Vanilla Bean Cafe

812 7th Avenue, Two Harbors, MN 55616
www.thevanillabean.com
Located on Hwy 61 just past the railroad underpass in Two Harbors.

Most Popular Foods: The huge **Oven Baked Omelets** for breakfast and their **Cranberry Club Sandwich** for lunch time favorite. The **Pan-Fried Walleye** has been a number one lunch and dinner choice since

the day they opened. They received the "Minnesota Monthly Critics Award" for their made-from-scratch soups. They use Minnesota-grown produce as seasons allow and about one-third of the menu is vegetarian. Their most popular dessert is the **Caramel Pecan Bread Pudding**, which began as a way to use leftover sweet rolls and became so popular that they now bake cinnamon/caramel/pecan rolls just for that dessert. They are broken up and baked in a sweet creamy egg custard, topped with their own homemade burnt sugar caramel sauce and whipped cream.

Vanilla Bean Cafe History: The "cute coffee shoppe name" was chosen for a bakery. When they found the "perfect" building to start their locally-owned family business, it had two front doors with one half already set up as a cafe, so they decided to give that a try, opening in May of 1998. The bakery faded while the cafe grew year by year through word-of-mouth. Folks stopped for coffee and a sweet only to discover the best full-service restaurant for miles around. They describe the cafe as "the best kept secret on the North Shore." While they struggle every day against the coffee shoppe name, they continue

JUDY'S CAFÉ

623 7th Ave, Two Harbors, MN 55616
218-834-4802
Located right on Hwy 61.

Most Popular Foods: Any **breakfast**, served all day long. A favorite would have to be the **Trout**—hash browns covered with cheese, smothered in sautéed onions and diced ham. The name originated from someone who use to cook at the place whose nickname was "Trout." Also popular their **all-you-can-eat walleye** on Friday evening (seasonal)—lightly breaded walleye deep-fried served with choice of potato and coleslaw made with a pineapple dressing. They make homemade pies and make daily specials with homemade soups.

Judy's Café History: John and Judy bought the restaurant in 1979. There was also a deli and bake shop located next to the cafe, which they also owned, but knocked down to make a bigger parking lot. They added on to the back of the kitchen and gave the cafe a face lift. For years, the cafe would serve a free Thanksgiving Dinner for those who had nowhere else to spend the holiday or couldn't afford it, but with rising food cost it had to stop in 2001. Judy's Cafe also used to do a lot of catering for years, but after that end of the business slowed down in 2003 or 2004 they decided it wasn't cost effective, though it is starting to pick up again. John passed away in early 1990s after battling heart disease, and Judy passed away in 2008 after years with lung cancer. Judy's Cafe is still owed and operated by family members and they hope can live up to John and Judy's legacy.

BETTY'S PIES

1633 Hwy 61 Two Harbors, MN 55616
www.bettyspies.com
Located three miles north of Two Harbors on Hwy 61

Most Popular Foods: Pies, Pie Shakes (ice cream, milk, and a slice of pie), **Pasties** (beef, chicken or veggie plus rutabagas, onions, carrots, potato), **Wild Rice Burger** (wild rice, flour, cheddar cheese, eggs, seasoning), and **Homemade Rye Bread**. Most popular pie is **Five-Layer Chocolate Cream** and **Great Lakes Crunch** (baked: rhubarb, apple, strawberry, and blueberry, raspberry).

Betty's Pies History: In 1956, Betty's father, Aleck, built a fish shack by the Stewart River on Highway 61. Betty thought it would be good to have some goodies for the fishermen, so she started making donuts and coffee. She began selling hamburgers and hot dogs. Customers didn't really like looking at dead fish while they ate, so, in 1958, Betty turned the fish stand into a cafe named Betty's Cafe. She added pies to her menu. Betty added a lunch counter and more seating, and the pie selection expanded too. In 1974, after more expansions, Betty changed the name to Betty's Pies. In 1984 after making thousands of pies, Betty sold the café and retired. In 1997, when Highway 61 was going to be expanded and the old restaurant needed to move or be rebuilt, the famous café was sold again to the current owners, Carl Ehlenz and Martha Sieber. The new building was opened May of 2000 bringing with it much of the atmosphere of the old building, which was torn down in the spring of 2002. They also opened a new Betty's Pies in Mahtomedi, Minnesota.

Lazy Moose Grille and Coffee House

300 Arrowhead Lane PO Box 447 Moose Lake, MN 5576
lazymoosegrille@yahoo.com
Approximately 2 miles from Hwy 61. From Hwy 61 take a left at the
3-way stop, go through town almost to second set of lights.
They are on the left.

Most Popular Foods: Chicken Salad Croissant (chicken with toasted
almonds, salad dressing, grapes)**, Homemade Meatloaf** and **Liver
with Onions**. Many more items to choose from, their menu is updated
quarterly with new items.

Lazy Moose Grille and Coffee House History: The owner is Dave
Lund, who built this building in 1989. It was called the Wyndtree. He
sold the Wyntree to Dave Hemmila in 2003, when it was called the
Blue Bear. Dave now has the restaurant back beginning in January 1,
2010, and renamed it the Lazy Moose Grille and Coffee House. Dave
and Janis Lund are
prominent business
people in this area.
They also own
Lakeside Traders, a
gift shop.

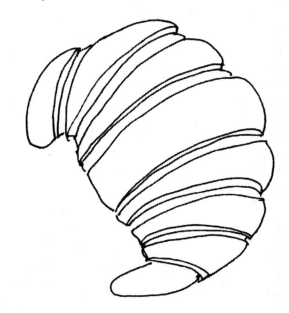

Peggy Sue's Café

8135 County Highway 61 Willow River, MN 55795
218-372-3935
Located on Highway 61.

Most Popular food: The **Taco Salad**—fresh salad greens inside a crisp taco shell, topped with seasoned beef, shredded cheese, tomatoes, olives, and green onion, served with salsa and sour cream.

Peggy Sue's Café History: The building was built in 1895. In 1924, Barney and Amy Amundson opened the Willow River Cafe confectionary. After Barney's death in 1944, the cafe was purchased by Bill and Viola Sedo. Vi's sister JoAnn recalls their price for a full pork dinner with pie and coffee being sixty-five cents. Successive owners were Wanda Poslusny and Les and Clara Proulx, who did extreme remodeling of the original building. Other owners included Phyllis Chapman, who named her ice cream parlor, The Glacerie; Patty Kaffer of Kaffer's Katering; and Eddie Mahren, Willow River Cafe. In 1993, Van and Jenny Thompson did complete renovation and brought back "real home cooking" as Van would say. Before Van's tragic death in 1995, his sister Peggy and her husband, Al Villa, took over. Today they continue the tradition of great food and friendly, small-town service.

THE VILLAGE INN

245 Third Avenue SE Pine City, MN 55063
"The Village Inn" is on Facebook   320-629-9942
Located 1.3 miles off Hwy 35W. Exit 169 east to Hwy 61 north
through town to Third Avenue. Go east over the tracks.

Most Popular Foods: Burgers — five ounces of fresh ground beef and the "Fat Man," (which has two five ounce patties), served with with bacon, mushrooms, Swiss and American cheese, potato chips or a basket of French fries and cole slaw, and **Tacos** (deep fried with the choice of chicken or beef and loaded with meat, lettuce, cheese, onions, and tomatoes). Enjoy with jalapeños and black olives upon request. Quoted on <www.urban spoon. com> that they have "the best tacos in town." "Saturday Tacos are out of this world." Guests also enjoy quesadilla's, nacho's supreme, or a taco salad also available in beef or chicken.

History of the Village Inn: In business since the late 1800s, it was located within two blocks of a lumberyard, a lumber mill, two hotels and the railroad depot. Today it is located within two blocks of two clinics, a nursing home, a feed mill, and TSA (counseling service). The Village Inn was first owned under the name Soderbeck in 1905. The sign reading "Buselmeier," (a beer the Village Inn was the first to carry and produced in the 1880s). Its brewery was located about two blocks away. Hamm's eventually bought the brewery. Today the old brewery is Fairview Lakes Clinic and a nursing home.

The bar was originally named Frank Womela Tavern, which also had a diner and barber shop. The Naval Miltia would meet there as they did not have a base.

The Village Inn today is owned by Danny Haavisto. The bar still has the original back bar from the late 1800s.

CORNERSTONE PUB & PRIME RIB

26753 Forest Blvd. Wyoming, MN 55092
www.cornerstonepubandprime.com
Right on Hwy 61 at the intersection of County Road 22.

Most Popular Foods: Prime Rib, Steaks, Chicken, Pork, Walleye and **Shrimp** as well as a variety of **Sandwiches** and **Salads**.

Cornerstone Pub & Prime Rib History: The Cornerstone Pub & Prime was the first stagecoach stop between St. Paul and Duluth and a hotel back in the 1920s. Sometime back in the 1940s, a gentleman died in one of the hotel rooms, and it was rumored that he was murdered. Some believe he haunts the Cornerstone Pub, and some have claimed to see him . . . they call him Freddie!

GULDEN'S RESTAURANT & BAR

2999 Highway 61 North • Maplewood, MN 55109
www.guldens61.com
Located on Hwy 61 and County Road D.

Most Popular Foods: Gulden's is a family-friendly restaurant serving American style cuisine including steak, chicken, pasta, seafood dishes, and homemade soups. Among their many popular lunch and dinner items, they are well known for their **Prime Rib, Sirloin Steak, Fried Chicken**, and **Walleye**. Their half-pound burgers and daily lunch buffets are also big hits among their customers.

Gulden's Restaurant & Bar History: Family owned and operated since 1934.

LAS MARGARITAS
MEXICAN RESTAURANT

2100 Vermillion Street Hastings, MN 55033
www.margaritas.comcastbiz.net
Located on Hwy 61

Most Popular Food: Puerto Vallarta Fajita, their special recipe of tender steak, chicken breast, shrimp, and chorizo cooked with sautéed onions, bell peppers, and tomatoes. Served with a quesadilla, Mexican rice, refried beans, cheese, pico de gallo, and lettuce.

Las Margaritas Mexican Restaurand History: Established December 31, 2002, it was founded by Hector Castro and his brothers-in-law Javier Perez and Juan Perez. Hector, born in California and raised in La Piedad, Michoacan, Mexico, wanted to make home-style Mexican food. He created a menu with authentic recipes and a great variety of dishes. He's had great success with his restaurant and opened a second location in Cottage Grove, Minnesota, in 2005.

THE BUSTED NUT BAR & GRILL

118 2nd Street East -Hastings, MN 55033
www.thebustednut.com
One block east of the Hwy 61 bridge on the
historic downtown main street.

Most Popular Food: — a generous portion of Minnesota Sunfish filets lightly seasoned and breaded, pan fried and served with steamed vegetables and wild rice.

The Busted Nut Bar & Grill History: Opened in 2004 as a peanut bar with a focus on great food, great service, and the coldest beer in town, the building was constructed in 1895 and has been the home of numerous businesses, including a dry goods store, a dress shop, and an ice-cream parlor. The Minnesota paranormal society (and some of their staff) believe they also have a ghost in residence here.

Bev's Cafe

221 Bush Street, Red Wing, MN 55066
www. bevscafe.com
One block off Hwy 61. Take a right at the Uffda Shoppe. They are on the left side of the street.

Most Popular Food: Biscuits and Gravy — a buttermilk biscuit smothered with homemade sausage gravy with big hunks of sausage in it. Served piping hot!

Bev's Cafe History: The oldest restaurant in Red Wing. The building was established in 1923. It has been a hardware store and had a bakery in the basement. Though it's had different names, it has been Bev's Cafe the longest. They celebrated their twenty-seventh anniversary on Valentine's Day 2010! They received the Restaurant of the Year award from the Chamber of Commerce for 2009!

LIBERTY'S RESTAURANT AND LOUNGE

303 West 3rd Street Red Wings, MN 55066
www.libertysonline.com
Located one block off Hwy 61

Most Popular Foods: Pizza, steaks, ribs, seafood, hamburgers, sandwiches, homemade soups — all popular. All their foods are made from scratch. Pizza, Ribs, USDA Choice steaks, seafood, great selection of sandwiches, and different variations of hamburgers and chicken sandwiches, Italian entrees, Mexican entrees, and kids' menu. They have a very extensive menu selection.

Liberty's Restaurant History: Started in 1975 by Lee and Dorothy Noreen, it opened just before the bi-centennial year . . . hence the name Liberty's. They started out in a small building about a block from their present location with just delivery and carry out. With the popularity of Liberty Pizza going wild, they outgrew the first building within the first year and moved to Main Street to a larger building which seated about seventy-five people. Along with the bigger building, they expanded the menu as well.

In 1984 Red Wing Shoe bought out the entire block where Liberty's called home. They moved to their present location on the corner of Third and Plum streets. With this move as well as the last, Lee and Dorothy expanded the menu, incorporating a full-service bar. The current location seats about 150 people. Their delivery, pick up, catering, dine in, and lounge are all still going today.

The current owner, the offspring of Lee and Dorothy, has worked at Liberty's since 1981 starting off doing dishes and busing tables and, in 1999, purchased the restaurant and is continuing the tradition of home-cooked meals and great service that made Liberty's what it is today. Many of the same recipes that mom and dad used back in the mid 1970s are still being used today. In fact, there has only been two people in the over thirty-five years that have mixed the secret recipe of spices together to make their pizza sauce, my father and myself.

It has been a great journey for their whole family running this restaurant in such a wonderful community like Red Wing. Becoming part of the history of Red Wing and being a destination in Red Wing has been an honor for us and will be for the many years to come.

SLIPPERY'S

10 Church Ave Wabasha, MN 55981
One mile from Hwy 61 on the west end of Main St.

Most Popular Foods: Slippery Burgers and **Walleye Sandwich**, a fresh walleye fillet hand breaded and fried golden-brown served with lettuce, lemon, and their homemade tartar sauce with a choice of side.

Slippery's History: A well-known establishment that started as a cabin and has built a reputation over the years for providing great food and spirits on the river, the bar and grill was referred to in the movies, "Grumpy Old Men" and "Grumpier Old Men." They even featured a Grumpy Old Men Festival the last weekend in February! Conveniently located on the west end of Main Street, right on the Mississippi.

VINIFERA VINE & DINE

260 West Main Wabasha MN, 55981
www.viniferarestaurant.com
Just blocks off Hwy 61 on the river in downtown Wabasha.

Most Popular Food: Their signature dish is their **Steamed Mussels** with white wine, garlic, shallot, and fresh basil. They feature European-inspired comfort food from the great wine regions of the world, and their food selections reflect the wine regions represented on their wall of wine. They promote local sustainable agriculture and work with local farmers whenever possible to supply fresh produce, lamb, pork, and buffalo. Their European-style dining means smaller plates to allow guests to enjoy a wider variety of choices from their ever-changing menu. Their wine selections are from small producers the world over, and wines in the restaurant are offered at retail prices.

History of Vinifera Vine & Dine: Opened in 2008 in Wabasha, Minnesota, by Michael and Debbie Murray-John of Minneapolis, Vinifera got its name from *Vitis Vinifera*, the Latin species name for all wine-producing grapes, and they keep the simple enjoyment of wine as its focus. Chef Michael Murray-John offers Italian, French, Spanish, and even the occasional Argentine or Portuguese inspired dishes all done with as much local produce as possible. The dishes are elegant but simply plated and portion size encourages people to share multiple courses.

The wines are small productions and sourced primarily from a local direct importer, so very few can be found in any retail store. "They are wines made to be enjoyed with food," says Murray-John, who tries to bring a sense of small-town Europe to the restaurant by offering unusual varietals and wines found in and around the villages producing the wines, but not often exported to the states. "People are discovering there is so much more than Chardonnay and Merlot, and they try to make these options accessible to be tried and enjoyed."

The wine list is not a printed sheet, but an invitation to explore the wall of wine to select a bottle to bring back to their table. The wines in the restaurant are offered at the retail price, with a modest five dollar service charge added if they are opened at the table.

Vinifera offers great views of the river whether dining outside on the patio, in the wine bar and retail area, or on the upper balcony which offers a more formal dining experience.

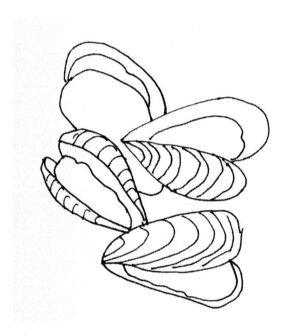

Steve's Anchor Inn

7110 Martina Rd., Goodview Minnesota 55987
stevesanchorinn@yahoo.com join us via stevesanchorinn/
facebook.com 507-474-4471
Right off of Hwy 61 N. From Winona before Minnesota City Exit.
From Hwy 61 S Wabasha after Minnesota City Exit.

Most Popular Foods: Dirty Taters (fresh vegetables and a variety of their breakfast meat piled on top of your choice of hashbrowns or homemade American fries, topped with a cheddar cheese melted on top and toast) and the **Reubens**. All of their food is homemade. Real potatoes and slow-cooked roasts that are extra tender and yummy! Their omelets are huge and come with potatoes and toast.

Steve's Anchor Inn History: Built back in the mid 1980s originally as a truck stop combined with the motel, there used to be showers and laundry facilities. It's been a few different restaurants, still a place for the locals and the tourists to eat. In 2007 a flood closed it down for nine weeks, but they pulled through and are doing great. Steve's is a family-run business and has a small crew but a big family with a big heart, and they can't wait to see more people enjoy the great eating at Steve's Anchor Inn!

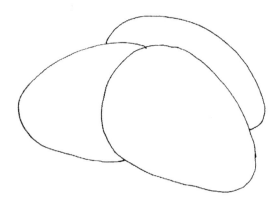

Chula Vista Mexican Restaurant and Cantina

1415 Service Drive Winona, MN 55987
www.chulawinona.com
Right off Hwy 61, less than half a block.

Most Popular Food: Chimichangas — deep-fried burrito with choice of ground beef or chicken, and covered with their housemade verde sauce.

Chula Vista Mexican Restaurant and Cantina History: Opened in 1988 to serve Mexican cuisine to Winona and the surrounding area, the food is made in-house daily, with their own secret blend of spices. They believe that Mexican food can be full of flavor without being "hot" to the palate.

US HIGHWAY 169

U.S. Highway 169 runs from Minnesota's Iron Range all the way south to Tulsa, Oklahoma. In Minnesota, it travels from the edge of the north wood Boundary Waters Canoe Area Wilderness through the Iron Range, skirts Lake Mille Lacs, cuts through Minneapolis' western suburbs, and then heads southwest, following the Minnesota River, passing through lush farmland to St. Peter and Mankato.

Along its way, Highway 169 touches on all Minnesota's main industries: lumber, mining, agriculture, higher education, and tourism. The Iron Range produced a large percentage of total iron ore for American manufacturing, and attracted a wide variety of immigrants to work in the mining industry.

Area sites include the U.S. Hockey Hall of Fame in Eveleth, the Iron Range Interperative Center and Minnesota Museum of Mines in Chisholm, the Ironworld Discovery Center and the Greyhound Bus Museum in Hibbing where the now-huge bus company had its start as a shuttle for miners. The town of Hibbing itself, where Bob Dylan grew up, actually had to move itself when the mining companies sought the ore right from underneath it!

Grand Rapids, once the northernmost port of call for Mississippi River steamships and later, birthplace of Judy Garland, has the Itasca Heritage and the Forest History Centers.

Mille Lacs is one of Minnesota's larger lakes. The Mille Lacs Indian Museum makes its home there, and a rest area built by the Civilian Conservation Corps overlooks the lake in Garrison.

In LeSueur, a statue of the Jolly Green Giant presides over a rich area of farmland.

Reference:

Barnard, R. Kent; 651-234-7504 Minnesota Department of Transportation.

The Great Minnesota Touring Book, Thomas Huhti. Trails Books, 2004.

Minnesota Department of Natural Resources http://www.dnr.-state.mn.us.

ELY STEAK HOUSE

216 East Sheridan Street Ely, MN 55731
www.elysteakhouse.com
Located on Hwy 169. In Ely, Hwy 169 turns into Sheridan Street. Ely
Steak House is right at the top of the hill in downtown Ely, MN.

Most Popular Foods: The **"Kick Butt" Steak** (a fourteen-ounce Top

sirloin "butt" steak—a huge cut of tender beef—served sizzling. Best enjoyed—"spank it" black and bleu with Cajun blackened seasoning and creamy bleu cheese) and the **"Bucky" Burger** (a full half-pounder cooked to your liking and topped with cheddar cheese, smoky bacon, grilled onion, and the famous "Bucky" sauce!). Customers come back year after year for these delicious selections and many more from chicken to seafood to vegetarian. Nothing tastes better after a trip into the BWCAW.

Ely Steak House History: Opened in 1997 with the intention of filling a nitch missing in the community, the owners, Duke and Scott, wanted to provide a place for people coming out of the wilderness to have a drink and a good steak. The friendly, accommodating staff and the largest beer selection in the region may also have something to do with the Steak House's success. People come not only for the delicious fresh food, but also for the free pool in the cozy lounge, bubble hockey, the karaoke on Thursday and Saturday nights, and the Open Mic Jam night on Sundays that features local musicians and people from all over the world.

THE CHOCOLATE MOOSE

101 N. Central Ave. Ely, MN 55731
218-365-6343
Located on Hwy 169, on the corner with Central — the first stop light

Most Popular Foods: Wild-rice-crusted Walleye (a large skinned fillet of walleye dredged in popped and milled wild rice and pan seared. Served with a proprietary homemade tartar sauce and fresh tomato and basil salad) and **Chocolate Moose Cake** (a deep dark chocolate and espresso mousse folded into a crust of homemade brownies).

History of the Chocolate Moose: Beginnings can be traced to the Scandinavian Ice Cream Shop founded by Barry and Milli Bissonett and Steve and Nancy Piragis in the spring of 1984. The following year the Chocolate Moose was born. Housed in a hand-scribed log building constructed of local red and white pine, the original restaurant was contained entirely in the log structure built on the site of the old Shagawa Hotel. Due to its success and the level of business during the summer, a new kitchen was constructed in 1987. In 1989 table service was introduced and a beer and wine license acquired. In 1998 Trish Bulinski purchased the restaurant, transforming to a full-service, scratch American Bistro satisfying a more sophisticated palette than is common in Nothern Minnesota.

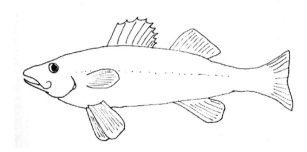

ADVENTURES RESTAURANT & PUB/CATERING

5475 Mountain Iron Drive Virginia, MN 55792
218-741-7151
Located on Hwy 53, about a five-iron south of Hwy 169.

Most Popular foods: Broiled Jumbo Shrimp, Elk Steak Tuscany, Ritz Walleye, and **Ultimate Bloody Mary**. They have a wide range of homemade soups, salads, burgers, sandwiches, steaks, seafood, ribs, pasta, vegetarian items, and desserts, and feature different ethnic and seasonal specials, such as Asian, Italian, German, Caribbean, and Mexican. They have a full bar and excellent wine selection. They also have catering and banquet options.

Adventures Restaurant & Pub/Catering History: Owner/operators Greg and Martha Hartnett opened the Virginia, Minnesota, location in 2002. The menu and décor reflect their lifestyle—active and outdoorsy—hence the name. A few accolades to their credit include the Entrepreneur of the Year Award from the Laurentian Chamber, Silver Plate Award from Best Independent Restaurants, and Certificate of Recognition as an Outstanding Foodservice Operation from the St. Louis County, Minnesota, Health Department.

THE IRON KETTLE
FAMILY RESTAURANT

601 3rd St. S.W. Chisholm, MN 55719
218-254-3339
Located about half a mile off Hwy 169. Turn into Chisholm at the
intersection with Hwy 73 where the eighty-five-foot Ironman statue
stands, follow Hwy 73. They are down the road on the left.

Most Popular Foods: There are twenty-five breakfast choices from
caramel rolls to oatmeal or waffles, nineteen sandwiches to choose
from, including the **Kettle Clubhouse Deluxe** and the **Chicken Bacon
Melt**, plus nine varieties of burgers including a **Double-Decker** with
bacon, **Patty Melt**, or **Jalapeno Burger**. Dinner ranges from **Stir-Fry** to
Steak and Shrimp, to **Smothered Chicken** and their **Double Pork
Chop Dinner**. An Iron Range tradition . . . the Friday night **Fish Fry**
where they serve a codfish nugget dinner with soup or salad and
choice of potato. Friday and Saturday nights' special also includes their
favorite **Prime Rib**. Their most popular food item has got to be their
Monroe Skillet, a golden brown bed of hashbrowns topped with two
eggs, sausage, onions, and green peppers served with choice of toast
or buttermilk pancakes.

Iron Kettle Family Restaurant History: Originally begun as a Country
Kitchen until the late 1980s, it was changed to the Iron Kettle Family
Restaurant in recognition of the mining industry that made this area
famous. Being in the heart of the Iron Range, they chose cozy, old-time
décor, reflecting days gone by and in memory of the struggle on the
Range miners went through to bring it to the great place it is today.
They also like to honor their servicemen and women who have served
to preserve their freedoms.

ZIMMY'S—THE ART OF FOOD & DRINK

531 East Howard Street, Hibbing, Minnesota 55746
Hwy 169 to Howard Street (historic downtown Hibbing) for five
blocks. They are on the right.

Most Popular Food: Oriental Chicken Salad (a signature salad —
sautéed fresh snow peas, green and red pepper strips, onion petals,
sliced mushrooms, chicken breast julienned, served on a bed of
lettuce, topped with roasted almonds, mandarins oranges, crushed
fried wontons, and diced red pepper and tossed with their homemade
oriental dressing, served with a fortune cookie, green onion, fresh
bakery bread and butter). Also try their **Homemade Chili, Highway
61 Pizza, Merlot Tenderloin Steak, Taos Grilled Salmon, Porketta
Sandwich,** and **Nasty New Yorker.**

History of Zimmy's: Once a Historic trolley station at the turn of the
century, now Zimmy's is Hibbing's favorite dining establishment,
featuring exquisite local cuisine; lunch, dinner, and late-night menus.
Bob Dylan memoribilia abounds, paying tribute to the local hero, so
whether on "Highway 61 Revisited" or just " Blowin' in the Wind",
Zimmy's is a must.

Uncle Bill's BBQ and Cafe

10 NW 5th Street Grand Rapids, MN 55744
218-326-1387
300 feet from Hwy 169

Most Popular Foods: Most delicious, almost-famous homemade **Soups** (all kinds but try the oven roasted potato soup with potato and roasted leak puree, garnished with aged balsamic vinegar and chopped scallion served with homemade garlic croutons) and specializes in **North Carolina BBQ, Texas BBQ, Southern BBQ, Beef, Pork, Ribs,** and **Chicken.**

History of Uncle Bill's BBQ and Café: Opened January 1, 2010, in the Old Central School that is on the National Historic Register and built in the late 1800s. As the name indicates, it was a school, but now houses several retail businesses and several nonprofit organizations. The Itasca Historical Society occupies the entire second floor and is a treat for those interested in the rich history of the area.

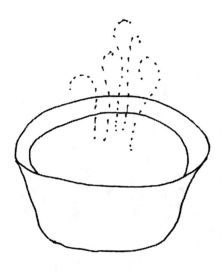

RIVERS ITALIAN

208 NE Third Street Grand Rapids, MN 55744
www.riversitalian.com
One block from Hwy 169.

Most Popular Foods: Contemporary Italian and French-influenced cooking. Menu changes frequently. Their food is sourced from local Minnesota farms and the best producers of quality farm-raised food using sustainable agriculture to ensure customers receive the best food, wine, and micro brews they can offer. Chef Matthew Taylor believes, "their plates should take direct inspiration from what is going on outside. Mother nature tells us what she is ready to have us cook." Everything in the Rivers Italian kitchen is handmade and produced fresh daily.

Rivers Italian History: Beginning in the winter of 2008 with the intention to bring fun and contemporary food paired with new and old world wines and the best craft beers they could find, to northern Minnesota. As Rivers began its journey, they found the most dedicated staff with the passion to bring a dining experience.

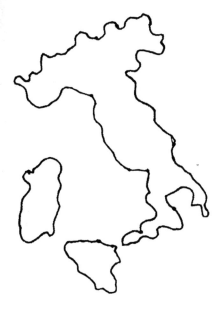

CORNER CLUB

Hwy 169 and Swatara Road Hay Point, MN.
218-697-9596
About seventy-five feet off Hwy 169

Most Popular Food: Fresh-Ground Hand-Pattie Burgers flame grilled to perfection with an assortment of toppings. Good Home Cookin' made with love . . . just like my grandma taught me!

Corner Club History: In 1929, the new Highway 169 was built from Aitkin to Hill City. This changed a lot of things for the area. The old Highway 35 had run through Swatara and on to Hill City. Now it ran through Haypoint. Frank Hutze moved his building to Haypoint in the early thirties and started the Corner Store. "Clifford Gravell owned the store from 1936 to 1940. After a couple of owners, Jack Jamme bought the store. He was there from about 1941 to 1954 with his son. Rick and Beth Jamme then bought the place and ran it until 1960. Beth Rice, Lyle Wagner, James Stone, and Herb and Doris Stansberry owned the place after that, and since August of 2009, it has been owned by Wes Catlin and Rebecca Drentlaw.

ROADSIDE FAMILY RESTAURANT

120 Minnesota Ave No. Aitkin MN 56431
218-927-2113
Two blocks north of Hwy 169 or two blocks north of stop lights in
Aitkin (Hwy 169 and Hwy 210)

Most Popular Foods: Homemade Caramel and Cinnamon Rolls and
Home-Baked Pies, Bakery all around.

The Roadside Family Restaurant History: a fixture in Aitkin for forty
years. Once known as the Sportsmans, which burned down, then was
rebuilt as Roadside Restaurant. The current owners have had the
restaurant for nineteen years.

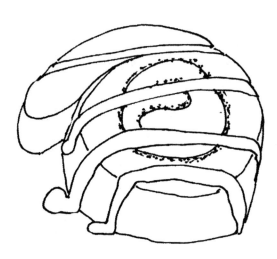

HAPPY'S DRIVE-IN

11373 Stevens Road Onamia, MN 56359
320-532-3336
Located on the North side of Highway 169.

Most Popular Food: Homemade Chicken Wild Rice Soup, a wonderful thick, creamy homemade soup with a perfect blend of Minnesota-grown wild rice, fresh vegetables, diced chicken, and select spices. Served in a soft herb bread bowl and topped with shredded cheddar cheese and seasoned croutons.

Happy's Drive-In History: Opened in May of 1990. There was no other restaurant like it in the area. The name Happy's came from family discussions. They started out with a small building that seated twenty-four people inside and about fifteen outside. Five years later a large seating area was added as well as an inside kids' play area.

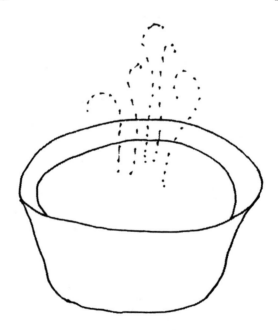

JIGGERS GRILL & BAR

130 Central Avenue South, Milaca, MN 56353
320-982-6283
Located within one mile of Highway 169 on Central Avenue

Most Popular Foods: Hand-Pattied Burgers and delicious **Sandwiches** as well as **Mexican** dishes. The **Enchiladas** are the biggest and best around. For their enchiladas they start with a ten-inch tortilla and stuff it with seasoned beef, cheese, and onions. It's covered with their special enchilada sauce and topped with cheese, onions, tomatoes, and black olives — or any combination — and served with Spanish rice and refried beans.

Jiggers Grill & Bar History: Under the current ownership for seven years, Jiggers has come to be known for their fantastic food, great service, and pleasant atmosphere. Jiggers has always been known to serve the best burger in town along with a wide assortment of other delicious food.

MERLIN'S FAMILY RESTAURANT

504 19th Ave. N Princeton, MN 55371
763-389-5170
Right on the corners of Hwy 169 and Hwy 95 in Princeton

Most Popular Food: Pancakes! Two plate-sized pancakes served with eggs and a choice of bacon, sausage, or ham. The **Big Stack** is for hungry people. Four plate-sized pancakes — if you finish them they will put your picture on the Big Stack wall and give you a free t-shirt saying "I ate the Big Stack!"

Merlin's Family Restaurant History: Started out in 1981 as Flapjack and a few years later changed to Merlin's, the current owners, Clayton and Sue Weitnauer, have been there since May 1994.

RISE N SHINE COFFEE AND DELI

12950 Fremont Ave #104 Zimmerman, MN 55398
763-856-1122
Located about one-half mile off Hwy 169

Most Popular Foods: Homemade Caramel Rolls and made fresh upon order sandwiches. Specialty coffees available as well, along with a long list of homemade desserts prepared daily. The deli offers a high stacked **Sassy Turkey** (choice of four delicious breads stacked with cream cheese, cranberries, walnuts, Swiss cheese, lettuce, onion, and turkey). In the mood for a warm sandwich? They have a spicy **Toasty Roasty** (choice of bread with chipotle mayonnaise, cheddar cheese, deli pickles, and hot roast beef). Besides carmel rolls, they have **Bear Claw** pastry, **Scotcheroo Bars** and so much more, plus twenty **Coffee** selections or **Chai Tea**.

History of the Rise N Shine Coffee and Deli: Established in Zimmerman several years ago, it's quickly becoming a well-known landmark in this resort community that boarders the Sherburne County Wildlife Refuge. Started by a coffee coinsure, his talent caused many local coffee lovers to quickly surface, incorporating this deli as a stop in their daily routine. Recently was taken to a new level by owner Ron Vaughn. The Rise N Shine has became a thriving meeting place for all to enjoy, reunite, and grow.

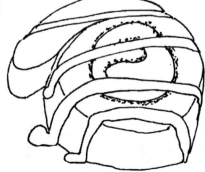

PAPA'S ITALIAN

26140 3rd Street East Zimmerman, MN 55398
www.papasitalian.com
Located one-half block off Hwy 169 at the stoplight in Zimmerman
behind Bremer Bank

Most Popular Foods: Smedly Pizza, Calzone, and **Spaghetti Pie.**
Their homemade dough is spread with their unique pizza sauce, then
topped with pepperoni, sausage, fresh mushrooms, green and black
olives, and the best cheese on the market (Grande Cheese). It's then
baked in a deck oven. The spaghetti pie is unique to Papa's Italian.
They also have **Alfredo Pies, Chili Pies,** and **Taco Pies.** They have the
best **Salads** around served with homemade dressings. Their sandwiches and subs are served on fresh-baked bread.

Papa's Italian History: Established in 1991 with the current family
taking over in 1996, the restaurant has always been a family-owned
business priding itself on its unique recipes. Everything is made from
scratch—the pizza dough, pizza sauce, spaghetti sauce, lasagna, as
well as many other types of pasta. The husband and wife owners work
the dining area, and their son works the kitchen making the food. A
Tuscany room was added in the last three years, giving seating for
eighty people.

SUNSHINE DEPOT

701 Main Street, Elk River MN 55330
www.sunshinedepot.com
One mile from Hwy 169 on Hwy 10

Most Popular Food: Pizza, the very best thin-crust homemade pizza.

Sunshine Depot History: The walls are covered with past and present sports athletes. While listening to some of Elk River's best sport stories guests can enjoy a tasty homemade pizza or a cold beer. From their lovely deck guests enjoy the view of the Mississippi.

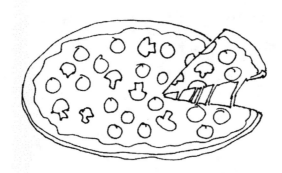

PABLO'S MEXICAN RESTAURANT

230 South Lewis Street, Shakapee, MN
www.pablosmexican.com
Two miles off Hwy 169

Popular food item: Enchiladas — soft, corn tortillas filled with a choice of filling and cheese, then topped with homemade enchilada sauce. Served with beans and rice.

Pablo's Mexican Restaurant History: The family moved from San Diego, California, to open Pablo's in 1986. They began in just a portion of their building and slowly grew into the space they now occupy. All of their entrees are made from scratch using selected recipes from Pablo's family heritage.

CLANCY'S BAR & PIZZA PARLOR

220 Triangle Lane North Jordan, MN 55352
www.clancyspizza.com
One block east of the Hwy 282/Hwy 169 intersection,
in the Triangle Business District.

Most Popular Foods: The **Burgers** (still hand pattied fresh every day). They offer a simple **Cheese Burger** or it can be "doctored up" to a **Double Rory Burger** (two patties, bacon, lettuce, tomato, mayo, Swiss cheese, American cheese, and mushrooms), the **Pizza** (the pizza sauce is my mother's recipe). Their basic ingredients — mild Italian sausage, pepperoni, Canadian bacon, and hamburger. Vegetables — black and green olives, onions, mushrooms, and green peppers. They also use pineapple. The **Audrey's Supreme** (named after my mother) is their top pizza), and the **Broasted Chicken** is great.

History of Clancy's Bar & Pizza Parlor: In the spring of 1982, Clancy (a laid-off airline worker) and Audrey (a waitress and hostess) parents of eight children, decided to purchase a bar with the intention of serving food. As the children grew, most worked at the establishment. It was a good fit for their sports-related family. Some of the food was named after members of the family. The Clancy Special and Audrey's Supreme (pizza), the Rory Burger, the Robin's Nest, and Randy's Sampler are examples.

As the times have changed, so has Clancy's. They evolved from a "bar with food" to a "restaurant with a bar." Randy and Rory (the two boys of the family) took over ownership in 2003 and have or had children working as cooks or bartenders or bussed tables since 2000.

OK Corral By Dangerfield's

20201 Johnson Memorial Drive Jordan, MN 55331
952-492-6700
Located along Hwy 169

Most Popular Foods: Fall off the bone **BBQ Ribs** — slow cooked with a flavorful blend of seasoning and their famous 1919 root-beer BBQ sauce. They serve **Beef Ribs**, bone-in **Country Style Ribs**, and **Baby Back Ribs.** Certified **Black Angus Prime Rib** is served after 4:00 p.m. Other meats include **Rib Eye, Pepper Steak, Filet Medallions, Pork Medallions, Chicken, Crab-stuffed Tilapia** and, of course, **Walleye** fried or broiled. They also have seven different **Salads.**

OK Corral by Dangerfield's History: The OK Corral was purchased recently by one of the top restaurateurs of the Twin Cities, Gus Khwice, owner of Dangerfields in Shakopee. A quick look around finds a large room with wooden floors, a lot of round tables and chairs, a big stone fireplace, and country chandeliers. Off to the right is another big room, then the bar room, a small side room called the Wyatt, a small party room, and a larger party room with its own bar and kitchen called the Tombstone. Their outdoor patio has its own wood-fired barbeque.

DUET'S

108 West Main Street Belle Plaine, MN, 56011
www.Duets.webs.com
Eight blocks from Hwy 169

Most Popular Food: Vivaldi Sandwich — smoked turkey, farmer cheese, green peppers, and mayo on a grilled tomato basil hoagie brushed with olive oil.

History of Duet's: Duet's is a family-owned business. Currently the owners are Rick and Mary Krant. A loved coffee shop of the Belle Plaine area, Duet's specialize in coffees, deli, and the gift department. Duet's has not always been a coffee shop, however. There is evidence that it was once a game room, mail office, old bar, and many other things.

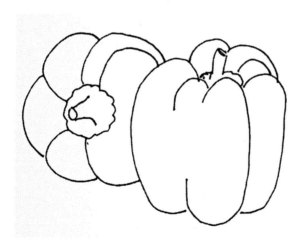

PIZZA RANCH

124 North 2nd Street, LeSueur MN 56058
507-665-2222
Located about two miles off Hwy 169.

Most Popular Foods: Pizza, Appetizers, and **Broasted Chicken** made to order. Full buffet includes a variety of pizzas, broasted chicken, mashed potatoes, gravy, cheese sticks, desert pizzas, salad bar, plus a beverage! Special feature buffet your way! Have a favorite pizza? They'll make it just for you to serve on the buffet!

History of the Pizza Ranch: Began in Hull, Iowa, in 1981, as an idea of Adrie Groeneweg, who was just nineteen years old, the first menu was developed by Lorraine Groeneweg, Adrie's mother, and included six specialty pizzas and single topping pizzas. The sauce and the dough were made from scratch, and the cheese grated by hand, while other ingredients were purchased or pre-made. People tried Pizza Ranch, and they loved it. Pizza Ranch grew. Today Pizza Ranch extends into nine states and is the largest regional pizza restaurant chain in Iowa, Minnesota, North Dakota, and South Dakota. They have been located in LeSueur for eight years, serving the community great food.

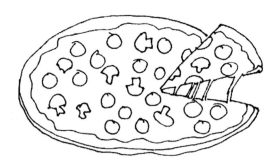

NEIGHBOR'S ITALIAN BISTRO

1812 S Riverfront Drive, Mankato MN 56001
www.neighborsitalianbistro.com
Two blocks off Hwy 169 on South Riverfront Drive in Mankato, just
south of Mankato West High School and the YMCA.

Most Popular Foods: Pasta, Fresh Seafood, extensive **Wine** menu. Pasta dishes, made from scratch with house-made sauces, fresh fish, and seafood selection, including Jurassic shrimp, crab, mussels, calamari, salmon, and more.

History of Neighbor's Italian Bistro: Opened in 2001 by brothers Patrick and Christopher Person, the former restaurant, Adrian's, was owned and operated for over thirty years by their parents until the brothers took over. The Neighbor's offers a complete menu with signature pastas made from scratch, grilled favorites, fresh salads, and more. The Neighbor's has won several community awards for "Best Italian Restaurant," "Best Ambiance/Atmosphere," and "Best Customer Service."

THE AMBOY COTTAGE CAFÉ

100 Maine Street East Amboy, MN 56010
www.amboycottagecafe.com
Located one-half mile east of Hwy 169

Most popular item: Raspberry Bread Pudding—homemade cinnamon rolls, organic flour, sugar, butter, milk and free range eggs go into their bread pudding and is topped with raspberries and whipped cream. Fresh daily and served warm, it has become their most popular dessert.

History of the Amboy Cottage Café: Demolition of this former 1928 cottage-style gas station was stopped by history-minded residents and the building relocated and renovated to continue service as an eating and gathering place for the community of Amboy. Owner Lisa Lindberg's traditional cooking focuses on healthy local food and sustaining a Minnesota small-town life style. Visitors seem to enjoy this tasteful step back in time.

BRICKHOUSE PIZZA

26 Main St. S., Winnebago, MN 56098
www.bagopizza.com
Located right on Hwy 169

Most Popular Foods: Chicken and **Ribs**. They serve fresh hot **Pizzas in varieties that many pizza places don't. They serve BBQ Chicken, Chicken Alfredo, Buffalo Chicken, Taco Pizza, Bacon Cheeseburger**, as well as the classic favorites.

History of Brickhouse Pizza: It is rather short. They opened late in 2009. It just didn't seem fair that small towns and rural areas could not have fresh, hot, great food delivered to them. So they solved the problem.

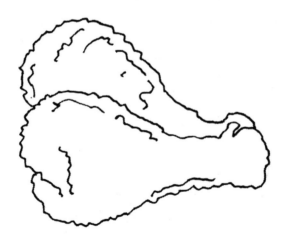

EL TIO RESTAURANT

224 N. Gove St. Blue Earth, MN 56013
507-526-4970
On Hwy 169 at 4th Street a few minutes from Hwy I-90.

Most Popular Foods: Enchiladas (soft corn tortillas filled with meat, rolled and covered with a mild homemade salsa, topped with lettuce, fresh cheese, and sour cream), **Tortas** (white bread — like a sub — filled with meat, onions, tomatoes, lettuce and avocados, and jalapenos when customers request them), **Tacos** (soft corn or flour tortillas filled with meat and topped with lettuce cilantro, onions, tomatoes and cheese on customers request), and **Plaza Fajitas** (a combination of chicken, shrimp, and beef cooked with onions, tomatoes and bell peppers served with a side of rice and beans and soft tortillas).

El Tio Restaurant History: Owned by a Mexican family that lived in Texas for many years, they moved to Minnesota and decided that this was a good place to raise kids, so they decided to stay and established the business in 2007. They offer take out and dine in. It is authentic Mexican food at reasonable prices.

Wildcat Café

203 Willis Street Elmore, MN 56027
507-943-3400
Located one block east of Hwy 169

Most Popular Foods: Big breakfast—two eggs, hash browns, choice of meat (bacon, sausage, or ham), and toast. They also have **Ham and Cheese Omelets** with hash browns and toast.

History of the Wildcat Cafe: It was a learning experience for students at Elmore Academy, students in need of help—education and work-based learning programs. The Wildcat Café opened in 2003, relocated in the old Elmore Eye building (newspaper) and has been there ever since. Their customers are very understanding of their students, knowing they have never worked in a café before. They continually have new students training. They are very eager to learn and please their customers, their hope is to help them get jobs when they leave Elmore Academy. Elmore, Minnesota, is the Home Walter F. Mondale and the gymnasium is named after him.

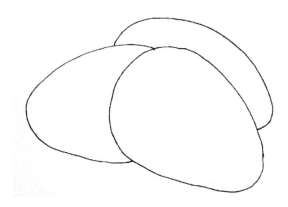

INTERSTATE 35

Interstate Highway 35 stretches from the U.S. border with Mexico at Laredo, Texas, all the way to Duluth, Minnesota. I-35 passes through Albert Lea, Owatonna, and Faribault, divides into two branches to traverse the Twin Cities, and then reunites to travel north through many of the towns that were once served by the passenger train to Duluth. The town of Hinckley is still a favorite halfway rest spot for northern travelers.

There's nothing quite like the ride north from the Twin Cities toward Duluth: after miles of flat farmland, marshes and lakes, birch and pine forests begin to appear. Later, rocky outcroppings can be seen, and the long rise begins that gives a picturesque view of the dense northern forests until finally, at the peak, the vista of Lake Superior and the Twin Ports of Duluth and Superior can be spotted.

Through St. Paul, I-35E was one of the last sections built in the interstate system, and thus benefited from rethinking and long negotiations to create a more aesthetically pleasing highway, enhanced by a lower speed limit.

In Minneapolis, I-35W gained notoriety on August 1, 2007, when its bridge over the Mississippi River collapsed, leading to thirteen deaths and many narrow escapes. A new bridge was built within a year.

In Duluth, I-35 was the last section of the national freeway system and was designed to fit the scenic Lake Superior shoreline, including a tunnel for a portion of it.

References:
Barnard, R. Kent; 651-234-7504 Minnesota Department of Transportation.
The Great Minnesota Touring Book, Thomas Huhti. Trails Books, 2004.
Minnesota Department of Natural Resources www.dnr.state.mn.us.

BURRITO UNION

1332 E. 4th Street Duluth, MN 55803
www.burritounion.com
Less than 5 minutes off Hwy 35, 4 blocks north and 14 blocks east of
the Lake Avenue exit in Duluth, MN

Most Popular Foods: Imperial Chicken Burrito — meal-sized burritos made from fresh ingredients and multi-cultural innovation. The **Imperial Chicken** is garlic-lime chicken with their seasoned rice, black bean medley, sautéed green peppers, and onions, plenty of cheese, roasted corn, and their spicy salsa.

History of the Burrito Union: They have been bringing friendly lunches, entertaining dinners and Fitger's Brewhouse Beer to Duluth for three years now.

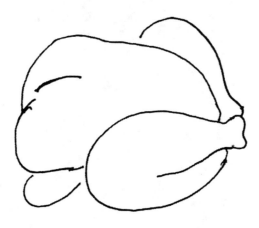

HELLBURGERS

310 Lake Ave South Duluth MN 55802
www.hellburgers.com   218-727-1620
Two blocks off Hwy I-35 (Exit on Lake Ave South)

Most Popular Foods: The **Original HellBurger**, a hand-pattied; one-third pound burger that can be customized with dozens of build-your-own options. Also **Jumbo Wings** in a variety of kickass sauces.

History of HellBurgers: A chef-owned, one-of-a-kind restaurant in Duluth's Canal Park, serving hand-pattied burgers, brats, wings, and award-winning food such as the Walleye BLT featured in *Gourmet Magazine* and Ham and Pear Crisp featured in *America's Ten Best Sandwiches.*

GORDY'S HI-HAT

415 Sunnyside Drive Cloquet, MN 55720
www.gordys-hihat.com
2.5 miles off Hwy 35 on Hwy 33 N

Most Popular Foods: Burgers (all are fresh hand-pattied USDA beef), **Fish Sandwich** (hand-battered Alaskan fish), **Onion Rings** (made fresh daily), **Shakes** and **Malts**.

History of Gordy's Hi-Hat: Native Duluthians Gordy and Marilyn Lundquist built the first A & W Root Beer stand in Eveleth, Minnesota, sixty years ago—1950. Customers, served by car-hops, enjoyed frosted mugs of root beer brewed on the premises, hand-pattied hamburgers on locally baked hamburger buns sliced by hand. Those were the good old days, when entertainment was piling the family in the car and heading out for homemade root beer or root beer floats. This was a seasonal business—open from Memorial Day through Labor Day. In 1955 Gordy and Marilyn built the London Inn Drive Inn on London Road in Duluth. It was a popular gathering place for all the Duluth high schools where they would drive in and sit on the hoods of their cars with radios blasting out Elvis or the Everly Brothers! They could get a hamburger, French fries, and a shake for fifty-seven cents! The London Inn was so busy the bakery would leave the bun truck loaded with buns for them. The hamburgers were all pattied by hand, and the French fries were peeled, sliced, and blanched fresh. In 1960 Gordy and Marilyn built Gordy's Hi-Hat in Cloquet, now in its fiftieth season. Still fresh hand-pattied burgers, homemade onion rings, hand-dipped fish and fresh-blended shakes. Gordy and Marilyn are both in their eighties and still active in the business.

GORDY'S WARMING HOUSE

411 Sunnyside Drive Cloquet, MN 55720
www.warming-house.com
Located 2.5 miles off Hwy 35 on Hwy 33 N

Most Popular Foods: Ice Cream, Lattes, Mochas, and **Chili.** Thirty-two flavors of old fashioned premium ice cream in dipped homemade waffle cones. Fresh steamed lattes and mochas made with their own rich locally roasted espresso blend. Their beef chili and white chicken chili are homemade.

History of Gordy's Warming House: Opened in 2005 in the remodeled old Lundquist home next to Gordy's Hi-Hat Restaurant, the ice cream parlor was moved into this building to make more space for additional ice cream and dessert items. A complete gourmet coffee and tea menu was added, with custom roasted coffees and drive-thru window. A huge deck and playground was added to service just about any age. Open year-round, a great community gathering place and pit stop for travelers going north or south, they are a halfway stop from Minneapolis/St.Paul to the northern lakes.

JOE JITTERS COFFEEHOUSE

308 Elm Avenue, Moose Lake, MN 55767
218-485-0660
Located 2.2 miles from Hwy 35W.

Most Popular Foods: Chicken Cashew Salad — mixed greens, piled high, topped with seasoned chicken chunks, cheese, cashews, craisins, and dressing. Served with grilled sourdough on the side. Other menu favorites include their healthy **Soups, Grilled Panini Sandwiches,** scrumptious **Muffins,** and **Scones.** They have a large variety of hot and cold **Coffee Drinks** and all-natural **Smoothies.**

History of Joe Jitters Coffeehouse: In December of 1999, the original owners, Doug Skelton and Curt Yort, after years of talking, purchased an old, historic building in the downtown, on Elm Avenue, which used to be the old Highway 61, which took travelers along the lakeshore of Moose Head Lake. Originally this structure housed the first Ford garage in the early 1950s.

Doug and Curt's goal was to provide high quality, healthy foods along with the freshest, locally roasted coffee grown and picked in a way to qualify it as the finest gourmet coffee in the world!

New owners, Randy and Ann Jusczak purchased the building and business in the fall of 2007. They have added high-speed Internet staying with the theme and integrity the original owners intended.

ARTS CAFE

200 Arrowhead Lane, Moose Lake, MN 55767
218-485-4602
Located 2.5 mile from Hwy 35.

Most Popular Foods: Hot Beef, Turkey, Meatloaf, and **Ham Sandwiches**, served with mashed potatoes and their homemade gravy covering it all! They offer homemade cakes at very affordable prices. Still serving coffee at forty cents for a bottomless cup.

History of Arts Cafe: Started in 1931 by the Abrahamsons and known as Dix Cafe, it became Arts Cafe when Art Jones owned it. Currently it's owned by Cheryl Fitzgerald, who worked at Arts ten years before purchasing in 2007. Arts has always maintained a home-town atmosphere, with homemade quality and great low prices

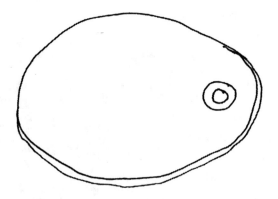

FINLAYSON CAFE

6501 School Street North Finlayson, MN 55735
www.finlaysonCafe.com
Located on Hwy 18 in Finlayson, 5 miles or 9 min NW of I-35

Most Popular Foods: The **Italian Omelet** (a three-egg omelet wrapped around a hearty helping of hashbrowns, American cheese, Italian sausage, onions, green peppers, and mushrooms) and the **Hot Beef** (slow-roasted beef sandwiched between two thick slices of bread and nestled between them is their real, hand-mashed potatoes, all covered with made-from-scratch gravy).

History of the Finlayson Cafe: was opened in 1998 by Dan Mayer, who started the reputation of their home-style cooking. He then sold it to one of his waitresses, Christine Molloy, who continued the quality of food and service for the next eight years. In November of 2007, Christine sold the cafe to Mark and Rachael Henkel, who, to date continue the high standards, operating the cafe as a gathering place for the local residents and a preferred stop for many on the way to Mille Lacs Lake.

Amy's Country Cafe

420 North Main Street PO Box 425 Sandstone MN 55735
Facebook @ Amy's country cafe. 320-245-2481
On Main Street by the bank and post office

Most Popular Foods: Breakfast — homemade from gravies to dessert. The **Supreme Hash Browns** — an extra large portion of hash browns with scrambled eggs cooked right in, with a choice of cheese or Sausage gravy, topped with a ham, onion, and green peppers. The Leeann Wrap (named after one of their cooks) is either grilled or crispy chicken in a large wrap with loads of cheese, tomatoes, lettuce, bacon onions and ranch dressing. Also known for their hot sandwichs — **Hot Beef, Hot Ma's Meatloaf**, and a **Hot Hamburger**.

Amy's Country Cafe History: The building was built in the 1920s as a saloon and a supplies store used by the quarry miners when the quarry was open. Several years later, a fire closed it until a local family opened a pizza place and bar in it. After the pizza place and bar closed, it was reopened as a cafe for sixteen years. The current owners purchased the cafe from the previous owners' daughter and run it as Amy's Country Cafe.

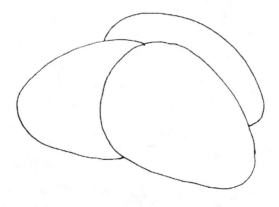

TOBIES RESTAURANT & BAKERY

404 Fire Monument Road, Hinckley, MN 55037
www.tobies.com
Located adjacent to I-35, at exit 183, in Hinckley

Most Popular Food: World Famous Caramel Rolls — their original dough recipe is swirled with cinnamon sugar and topped with Tobies own rich caramel. Delicious!

Tobies Restaurant & Bakery History: The café began serving its donuts and coffee in 1920 with Mr. and Mrs. Isodore Wendt as proprietors for the next twenty-seven years. April 1, 1947, Mr. and Mrs. "Tobie" Lackner took over, changing the name to "Tobies Eat Shop & Bus Stop." In 1966, after nineteen years as owners, Tobie and Ann decided to retire. I-35 came through, which meant relocation. Mr. and Mrs. John Schrade moved this thriving eatery to its new freeway location in 1966. Today second and third generation family maintains the same friendly atmosphere everyone has come to know.

THE BEBOP VENUE

1009 109th Ave NE, Blaine, MN 55434
www.thebebopvenue.com
Located just three miles west of 35W off Hwy 65
and 109th Ave in Blaine, MN.

Most Popular Food: The Big Bopper, a half pound fresh Angus burger topped with melted Swiss cheese and American cheese, two crispy strips of bacon, sautéed onions, and mushroom, lettuce, tomato and Secret Bebop Sauce. Served on a sesame pub bun.

The BeBop Venue History: Built in 1991, they have three softball fields, seven volleyball courts, and twelve horseshoe pits. The BeBop Venue has a fun atmosphere for sports or a night out. Their staff is always friendly and quick to serve you.

RAINFOREST CAFE

102 South Avenue, Bloomington, MN 55425
www.rainforestcafe.com
Just two miles east of Hwy 35W on Hwy 77 in the Mall of America

Most Popular Food: Sparkling Volcano, a giant, rich, chocolate brownie cake stacked up high, served warm with vanilla ice cream, fresh whipped cream and topped with caramel and chocolate sauces.

History of the Rainforest Cafe: A wild place to shop and eat! Discover the most realistic indoor rainforest ever created, complete with cascading waterfalls, lush vegetation, tropical rainstorms, aquariums, trumpeting elephants, and entertaining gorillas.

SAWATDEE THAI RESTAURANT

8501 Lyndale Avenue South Bloomington,MN 55420
www.sawatdee.com
Located about three blocks from Hwy 35

Most Popular Foods: Supenn's Fresh Spring Rolls (stuffed with shrimp, barbecued pork, crisp fresh vegetables, and noodles. Not deep-fried!) and the **Holy Basil Supreme** (stir-fried onions, mushrooms, hot or green peppers enhanced with sweet basil leaves, plus choice of tofu, chicken, beef, or shrimp). Enjoy some **Thai Ice Tea**, too.

History of Sawatdee Thai Restaurant: Begun in 1983 as the first Thai restaurant in the five-state area, Minnesotans were intrigued by the sweet, sour, bitter and salty combinations found in authentic Thai cooking. Over twenty-one years, Sawatdee has become a twin cities favorite. Multiple locations.

Jensens Cafe

12750 Nicolette Ave. Burnsville, MN 55337
www.jensenscafe.com
About ¼ to ½ mile off of 35-W.

Most Popular Food Item: Swedish Pancakes, large flat pancakes, much like a crepe, only with more flavor. They come with their homemade butter, maple syrup, and lingonberries or fresh strawberries and homemade whip cream.

Jensens Cafe History: They are a casual cafe that serves breakfast, lunch and dinner. They serve breakfast all day. In the Heart of Burnsville, on the corner of Nicolette and Burnsville Parkway, the ambiance is warm and inviting.

ROASTED PEAR

14200 Nicollet Ave, Burnsville, MN 55337
www.roastedpear.com or www.rpcatering.com
One-half mile from both 35E and 35W, between them just north of
County Rd 42 on Nicollet

Most Popular Food: Roasted Pear Spinach Salad—spinach, roasted pears, caramelized pecans, gorgonzola cheese, and balsamic vinaigrette.

History of the Roasted Pear: Founded in 2003, Roasted Pear is a family-owned, full-service bar and restaurant in Burnsville, Minnesota. Often described as elegant and casual, rustic and refined, the menu offers sophisticated salads, appetizers and brick-oven pizzas along with hearty pastas and meaty ribs and steaks.

HARRY'S CAFE

20790 Keokuk Ave Lakeville, MN 55044
www.eatatharrys.com
Overlooking I-35

Most Popular Food: Monte Cristo — three slices of French toast filled with generous portions of ham, turkey, bacon, tomatoes, cheddar and Monterey Jack cheeses, and topped with powdered sugar. Served with a side of sweet raspberry mayonnaise upon request.

History of Harry's Cafe: When Harry decided to open a restaurant, he chose not to purchase a franchise, instead designing it around his personality and high standards. Mostly from scratch, including the ice cream, soup, sauces, and salad dressings, Harry uses the highest quality and freshest ingredients. Produce and dairy are delivered throughout the week, and meats are delivered daily from a local butcher, as is their bread from a local bakery. He tries constantly to evolve and improve his menu and atmosphere.

RUDY'S REDEYE GRILL

20800 Kenrick Avenue Lakeville, MN 55044
www.rrglakeville.com
Visible from the freeway going south. Approximately half a mile
from the freeway entrance, one block north of County Road 70, east
of I-35, along the Kenrick Avenue Frontage Road and adjacent to the
Holiday Inn Hotel and Suites in Lakeville.

Most Popular Foods: Pan Fried Walleye (a four-ounce Canadian walleye fillet dredged in Ritz cracker crumbs, pan fried in butter and
topped with a compound butter and toasted almonds, then garnished
with a lemon wedge) and **Bull Bites** (eight ounces of beef tenderloin
tips coated with signature Cajun seasoning, then blackened in a cast
iron skillet. Prepared medium-rare, topped with diced plum tomatoes
and served on a bed of onion straws with a two-ounce ramekin of béarnaise sauce and another of horseradish cream sauce).

History of Rudy's Redeye Grill: From the 1950s to the 1970s when
Axels in Mendota was known as the Parker House, Linda Young's parents, Jeanette and Axel Lofgren, worked for Doughery's. Jeanette was
the kitchen manager, and Axel (who passed away twenty-seven years
ago) was the maintenance man. Linda began working at the Parker
House at the age of eleven, along with many friends and family. After
high school, she worked for Gannon's, Champps, and Byerly's.

Charlie Burrows also grew up in the restaurant business, as a
"soda jerk" at A&W, later for Left Guard (which became ChiChi's), the
Ediner, Two Peso's, Ciatti's, Champps, Ol' Mexico, and Byerly's.
Charlie also managed the Parker House under Jim Toye. During the
reconstruction of the Mendota Bridge, business fell, and Toye closed.

Linda and Charlie met working at Champps, and crossed paths
at Byerly's. They both had dreams of their own place. On July 1, 1996,
they opened Axel's River Grille, named after Linda's father Axel.

Charlie and Linda, along with the help of Mike Gayland, allowed their ventures to grow over the last several years to include five Axel's—Mendota, Chanhassen, Woodbury, Loretto (franchise), and Roseville (franchise); five Bonfire restaurants—Eagan, Woodbury, Grand Avenue, Savage and Blaine; and five Rudy's Redeye Grills—Rosemount, White Bear Lake (franchise), Alexandria (franchise), Steven's Point, Wisconsin (franchise), and Lakeville (franchise), as well as numerous concepts and franchises under development.

The Lakeville Rudy's Redeye Grill is a franchise store. This means they are operating under the Rudy's Redeye Grill name, using their concept, values and recipes, but they are not owned by Charlie and Linda. Rudy's in Lakeville is independently owned and operated by Forbears, LLC.

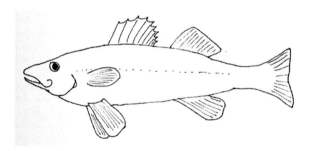

THE OLE CAFE

1011 St. Olaf Ave, Northfield MN 55057
www.the-ole-cafe.com
Seven miles from Hwy 35 on Hwy 19 in Northfield.

Most Popular Food: Pizza, many different types of pizza — nine inches in size and a thin crust. Called gourmet pizzas because of the use of fresh ingredients and the wide variety. The most popular: **Greek Pizza**, their **Sausage and Mushroom**, and also their **Barbeque Chicken**.

The Ole Cafe History: Opening May 2008, this cafeteria-style eatery offers a wide variety of soups, salads, build-your-own sandwiches, panninis, and, during dinner hours, build-you-own-pasta bar. They have a retail bakery, a pizza bar, and a coffee shop.

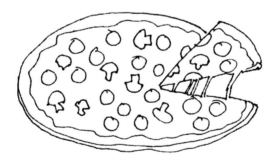

THE CONTENTED COW PUB

302B Division Street Northfield, MN 55057
www.contentedcow.com
Located just seven miles east of I-35 off exit Hwy 69

Most Popular Foods: Shepherd's Pie and **Spinach & Artichoke Dip** (made with three cheese and served with bread). Their **Nachos** are tortilla chips piled high with mixed cheese, pico de gallo, salsa, and sour cream. The menu also includes a variety of soups and sandwiches.

History of the Contented Cow Pub: Built in 1876 and bought by Norman Butler and Diane Burry in May 1999. Remodeled, it opened on the first day of the Defeat of Jesse James Days (DJJD), early September 1999. They knocked down the old jail building in 2001 to create a split level patio and added a deck in 2004. The lower patio was enclosed in 2007 to increase the available space inside the pub and they intend to add yet another deck in spring 2009.

The motto of the town is "Cows, Colleges, and Contentment," which led to the name. They were the first non-smoking establishment of its kind in Northfield, probably in the State (the USA?). They have no televisions, electronic games, pull-tabs, bar stools, or crap beer—just good domestic craft beers and imports on tap; they started with eight taps and now have thirteen. Their food is simple, mostly homemade and nutritious, and they pride themselves on being family-friendly.

BERNIE'S GRILL

129 Central Avenue North Faribault, MN 55021
www.vintageroom@hotmail.com
Located about three miles from I-35.

Most Popular Foods: Hashbrowns as ordered in the **Bernie Special** — choice of two eggs, homefries, hashbrowns or fresh fruit, sausage, bacon or ham and toast, pancakes, blueberry cheese pancake, or French toast .

History of Bernie's Grill: Opened in 1995 and relocated to their current spot in downtown Faribault, they renovated a historic building back into a ballroom (located on the third floor) with hotel suites on the second floor. The restaurant is on the main floor and caters to diverse group of people from the area.

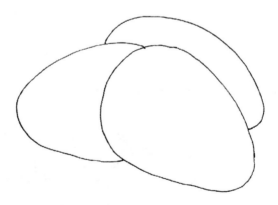

TOREY'S RESTAURANT & BAR

685 W. Bridge Street Suite #5 Owatonna, MN 55060
www.toreys.net
Located one block east of the Owatonna Bridge Street exit off I-35

Most Popular Food: Ribeye Steak — sixteen ounces of hand-cut choice center-cut ribeye char broiled and served on French fried onions.

History of Torey's Restaurant & Bar: Doors opened on February 1, 2001, by Chef Torey Statlander. Besides the restaurant and bar, Torey's offers full service catering.

MAGGIO'S PIZZA AND MISTYC PIZZA

Maggio's Pizza - 301 5th Avenue West Ellendale, MN 56026
Mistyc Pizza - 140 Main Street N Lonsdale, MN 55046
507-688-1050 (Ellendale) and 507-744-3688 (Lonsdale)
The Ellendale location is about one mile off I-35 to the west on Hwy 30 in the downtown. The Lonsdale location is eight miles off I-35 in downtown Lonsdale.

Most Popular Food: Homemade Pizza They make their own dough, unique due to a small amount of whole wheat flour. The sauce is also homemade with a blend of special seasonings. Vegetables are fresh; all onions and green peppers cut fresh daily, and they use fresh mushrooms.

History of Maggio's Pizza and Mistyc Pizza: Venturing into the pizza business six years ago was the owners first experience owning a restaurant and at a time when their kids were little so one of could be at home with the kids, who had a fun time helping out as much as they could. After a couple years in Ellendale, they opened a second store in Lonsdale, Minnesota. Both have family settings with room for parties, and they also have carry out and delivery.

GEORGES OF GENEVA

116 Central Avenue North Geneva, MN 56035
www.georgesofgeneva.com
Located two miles off the Geneva exit of I-35 going east.

Most Popular Foods: Chicken Dinner (four pieces broasted chicken served with choice of potato, coleslaw and Texas toast) and **Bar-B-Que Rib Dinner** (a full rack of bar-b-que ribs in their own homemade sauce, served with choice of potato, slaw, and Texas toast).

History of Georges of Geneva: Built as the Cottage Cafe in 1949 by Warren Wayne and Donald Gries, Leonard Giles owned it from 1951 to 1955 with the same name. From 1955 to 1963, Sam and Dorothy Worrell owned the Cottage Cafe. In 1963, Elwood Jensen purchased it, and ran the Cottage Cafe until 1986. Dave Newgaurd then purchased it, called it the Geneva Steakhouse and ran it until 1997. George Stieglebauer bought it and opened up as Georges of Geneva from 1997 until 2007, when Steve and Jodie Dittrich purchased and still own it as Georges of Geneva as of 2010.

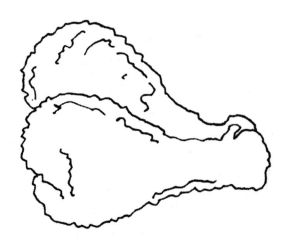

THE POUR HOUSE BAR & GRILL

102 Commercial Ave. Clarks Grove, MN 56016
On Facebook   507-256-8014
Located ¼ mile west of I-35, Exit 18, Clarks Grove, MN

Most Popular Foods: The **Pour House Burger** (grilled one-third-pound burger topped with two cheeses, mushrooms, bacon on a toasted bun) and the **Pour House Philly**.

History of the Pour House Bar & Grill: Originally founded as the Bulldog Bar and Grill in 2000, it's located in a building originally a set-ups bar and gas station. Converted to a bar and grill and opened for business in 2000, it's a popular spot with full-service bar and competent menu, including a kids menu and meal baskets.

US HIGHWAY 10

A sk many Minnesotans about their favorite summer place and they'll say, "You take Highway 10 . . ." This workhorse highway grew in part from oxcart trails in the 1800s that carried bison pelts and meat. It was partially paved by the 1920s. Today's mostly divided, four-lane highway still carries farm goods from the fertile Red River Valley, as well as vacationers seeking out the numerous summer festivals and craft fairs, camping, resorts — and that one perfect, big fish.

Stretching 270 miles across Minnesota, U.S. Highway 10 actually starts in Bay City, Michigan, and runs straight west to Lake Michigan — where the ferry provides a link — and then travels across Wisconsin. It's one of the few highways in the country to have a water link.

In Minnesota, Highway 10 passes from the Wisconsin border into St. Paul before traveling along I-35E, I-694 and I-35W and breaking off in the northern Twin Cities suburbs on its trip to the North Dakota border at Moorehead. Before the construction of the interstate freeway system, Highway 10 ran all the way to Seattle — its even-numbered designation indicates its east-west alignment.

Minnesotans use Highway 10 to get to and from Fargo-Moorehead, Detroit Lakes, Little Falls, St. Cloud, St. Paul, with important branches to Brainerd and Bemidji.

Besides some of the richest farmland in the country (the topsoil can go down five feet) and the popularity of the many lakeside resorts (the lakes being the remains of the last glacial period), the small towns along the route such as New York Mills, Motley, and Staples, produce many high school basketball championship teams.

Reference:
Barnard, R. Kent; 651-234-7504 Minnesota Department of Transportation
The Great Minnesota Touring Book, Thomas Huhti. Trails Books, 2004.
Minnesota Department of Natural Resources http://www.dnr.state.mn.us

Hi-Ho Tavern

10 Center Avenue Dilworth, MN 56529
218-287-2975
Located directly on Hwy 10

Most Popular Food: Hi-Ho Special — a high-quality fresh-ground daily all-beef patty prepared to order with raw or fried onions and topped with a toasted buttered bun, cheese, and pickles (other condiments optional). The Hi-Ho Special comes with a generous portion of golden French fries and a beverage (the fries and soda are unlimited).

History of the Hi-Ho Tavern: First opened in 1947 and owned by Glen Tollefson, for thirteen years it served only 3.2 beer and burgers. In 1960 Edith and Earl Cariveau bought the Hi-Ho and the family has run it ever since. In 1977 Rick and Cathy Cariveau took over for his parents and have opened the Hi-Ho South in 1996 and started serving burgers at the Newman Outdoor Staduim for Redhawks games since 2006. They are looking forward to the third generation of Cariveaus running the Hi-Ho with Rick and Cathys son Rick and his wife, Jamie, soon taking over. Although new things are added and new options are available, the Hi-Ho Special has proven to be a timeless classic.

ALTONY'S ITALIAN CAFÉ

4 Center Avenue West Dilworth, MN 56529
218-287-5557
Located directly on highway 10.

Most Popular Food: Spaghetti served with a salad, bread, and a small dish of soft-serve ice-cream. The plate has a generous portion of spaghetti noodles lightly coated with Al's homemade sauce. Each serving is topped with additional sauce and two large meatballs. The sauce and meatballs are made fresh daily. There is no sauce recipe except the season-and-taste-till-perfection method. The meatballs are made from freshly ground meat daily and seasoned with Italian spices. The size of the meatball is also important; each weighs at least a quarter pound and is perfectly shaped. The meatballs are simmered in the sauce all day, and the flavor tops off that of the homemade sauce.

Altony's Italian Café History: Opened July 2006 with the original thought for the restaurant to be an ice-cream shop selling hot-dogs and hamburgers, in the small Dilworth building that used to be Al's uncle Tony's Liquor store/Ice Cream Shop. In the days when ice-cream cones cost a nickel and "walk-up" windows were in style, the building served many customers. Once the work began for the new cafe, the idea of an ice-cream shop selling hot-dogs and hamburgers soon turned to "Let's put the things you're good at cooking on the menu and leave the hot-dogs and hamburgers to others." Soon Altony's was founded with the entire menu turning to Italian cuisine. Al's grandparents come from Italy in the early 1930s and ran a small Italian restaurant/nightclub in the Dilworth area for many years. The creation of Altony's followed that Italian heritage.

WHISTLE STOP CAFE

613 6th St. North Hawley MN 56549
218-483-4648
Located four blocks north of Hwy 10 on 6th St.

Most Popular Foods: Cajun Tuscan — pasta cooked to order, fresh garlic and Italian sausage with vegetables pan fried with Cajun seasoning. Served with garlic bread stick and shredded parmesan — and **Coconut Cream Pie** — creamy with excellent texture, refreshing for any season or any occasion.

History of the Whistle Stop Café: a converted black smith shop in 1980s formed the main body of the restaurant, and the new addition was an old jewelry store. They kept the full-size safe, which will be housing a small selection of wine and beer.

THE FIRESIDE

1462 East Shore Drive, Detroit Lakes, MN 56501
www.firesidedl.com
Located three blocks from Hwy 10

Most Popular Food: The Hand-Cut Prime Steaks. An immense dose of style dominates a menu filled with classic, eclectic and inventive fare.

History of the Fireside: Opened as a restaurant in 1948, it has been the staple of fine dining for Detroit Lakes and Becker County for over sixty years. Situated on 300 feet of lake front, the Fireside has a spectacular view of Lake Detroit and its wonderful sunsets.

SPEAK EASY RESTAURANT AND LOUNGE

1100 North Shore Drive Detroit Lakes, MN 56501
www.speakeasydl.com
Located one block south of Hwy 10

Most Popular Food: Blackened Chicken Rigatoni, a signature blend of sundried tomatoes, fresh mushrooms, and minced garlic, sautéed together with their house blackened seasoning, resting on a bed of rigatoni noodles, and finished with a blackened chicken breast, Alfredo sauce, fresh shredded parmesan, and garnished with red and green peppers.

History of the Speak Easy Restaurant and Lounge: Originally started in Moorhead, Minnesota, by the Mercil family thirty years ago. Twenty years later marked the expansion into the lakes area. Being a family-run business focuses attention on community and fellowship, setting us apart from larger corporations and chain restaurants. Keeping with the name, the atmosphere recalls the Roaring Twenties, complete with the getaway car!

SPANKY'S STONE HEARTH

34785 County Hwy 4 Vergas, MN 56587
www. spankysstonehearth.com.
Located three miles from Hwy 10 (Frazee Exit). Also 10 minute from
Detroit Lakes and Perham.

Most Popular Food: Stone Hearth Trio — New York Strip paired with
Pan Fried Sea Scallops and Pina Coloda Shrimp — dry-aged chef choice
strip loin prepared over hickory charcoal paired with fresh sweet sea
scallops on a bed of sautéed spinach, drizzled with house made
raspberry beurre blanc and jumbo pina colada shrimp over grilled
pineapple.

History of Spanky's Stone Hearth: Established in 1946 on the shores
of Rose Lake three miles northeast of Vergas Minnesota, the restaurant
has been a dining destination in the heart of the lakes area for countless
years. A white pine log lounge and deck were added in 1996. They
support local farmers and purchase locally grown and produced
products as much as possible. It's where passion meets innovation.

PIZZA RANCH

121 2nd Ave SE, Perham, MN 56573
www.pizzaranch.com
Located about a mile off Hwy 10 in downtown Perham

Favorite foods: Buffet, featuring most of the items on their menu —
pizza, chicken, appetizers, potatoes, gravy, and salad bar.

Pizza Ranch History: Began in Hull, Iowa, in 1981, as an idea of Adrie
Groeneweg, who was just nineteen years old. Today Pizza Ranch
extends into nine states and is the largest regional pizza restaurant
chain in Iowa, Minnesota, North Dakota, and South Dakota. Over the
years, changes have been made to virtually every aspect of Pizza
Ranch's products, services, and operations. Because guest satisfaction
is one of the focal points at Pizza Ranch, they continuously make
changes to increase consistency, efficiency, quality, and selection.

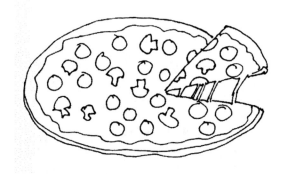

EAGLES CAFE

31 North Main, New York Mills, MN 56567
218-385-2469
Located in downtown New York Mills on the corner of Park St and
Main Ave, approximately one-half mile from Hwy 10,
almost under the water tower.

Popular Food: Homemade Pie — homemade, not just home baked! All
the pies use an old fashioned pie crust consisting of flour, lard, salt,
and water. All the cream fillings are cooked from scratch, and all fruit
pies are made from fruit, sugar, flour, — NEVER canned filling!

History of Eagles Cafe: The Gerber family purchased the Eagles Cafe
in June of 1984 from Wayne Erickson who started the cafe in the late
1970s. Orv and Jeanne ran the cafe until 1990 when they were joined
by their son Tom. Orv, Jeanne, Tom, and his wife, Julie, ran the cafe
until January 2002 when they sold it to Russel and Rhonda Peterman.
Tom and Julie repurchased the cafe in March 2006 and haven't left
since. They built their house on the back of the cafe in October 2006.

NITEOWL RESTAURANT & LOUNGE

1034 Ash Avenue NE, Wadena, MN 56482
218-631-3516
Immediately off on the North of Hwy 10.
The building itself is about 100 yards from Hwy 10.

Most Popular Foods: Homemade Pizza, Broasted Chicken, and **BBQ Ribs**. The home-made thin crust pizza is made from scratch. They make their own dough and their own sauce and top it generously with the best toppings.

History of the Niteowl Restaurant & Lounge: Around for approximately twenty-four years, George and Jil purchased the restaurant on January 1, 2006.

YESTERYEAR'S ICE CREAM CAFÉ

112 South Farwell St. Verndale MN 56481
218-445-5143
Located just one and a half blocks of Hwy 10

Most Popular Foods: Breakfast, Chicken and **BBQ Ribs**. A wide variety of breakfast specials, presser-cooked chicken, and their homemade BBQ sauce.

History of Yesteryear's Ice Cream Café: Scott and Susie have owned this small town café for over twenty years and have offered home-cooked meals at affordable prices with a great atmosphere for the whole family.

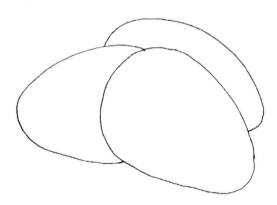

THE SPOT CAFE

116 2nd Ave NW Staples MN 56479
218-894-9928
Located on Hwy 10 on the west end of town.
Look for the big red SPOT flasher on the sign

Most Popular Food: Omelets — started with fresh-diced ingredients like ham, bacon, sausage, onions, tomatoes. Then hand-cracked eggs are whipped into a frenzy to create a fluffy, light omelet. Cheese smothers the ingredients before they are rolled up. Paired with hashbrowns and a choice of toast.

History of the Spot Cafe: With beginnings over thirty years ago, the Spot Cafe has shown what "Minnesota nice" really means. It continues to be a gathering place for seniors and families around the Staples, Motley, Lincoln area. They have multiple coffee clubs that meet every day so if you need a drinking buddy just stop on by. Family-owned and operated, the Spot Cafe offers a menu to satisfy any hungry traveler.

COUNTRYSIDE RESTAURANT

880 U.S. 10 Motley, MN 56466
218-352-6777
Located just south of Motley right on Hwy 10

Most Popular Foods: Large hand-pattied **Burgers, Beef** and **Turkey** roast right from the oven, and daily **Soups** made from scratch are some of their offerings. The loaded **Three-Egg Omelets** have diced meats and vegetables, shredded American cheese, fresh hashbrowns, and a choice of fluffy pancakes or toast.

Countryside Restaurant History: In Motley for over ten years, some of the original staff continue to serve guests with a smile. The Motley Countryside was the fourth and final one built. Over the years, each has become independently owned and operated. The menu was originally created with the goal was to offer homemade recipes "just like grandma used to make." Most of the ideas for the menu have been a huge success. But, the biggest, most important standard here is, no short-cuts. Fresh food tastes better.

THE LANDING RESTAURANT
AT LAKE ALEXANDER

7832 Copper Road Cushing MN 56443
218-575-3015
Located on Hwy 1, eight miles North of Randall and Hwy 10 or 18
miles from the Hwy 371 and Hwy 10 split after Little Falls.

Most Popular Foods: Crab Baked Walleye Pike (walleye pike topped with fresh lump crabmeat, broiled and served with a basil butter sauce), **Traditional Veal Liver** (sautéed tender veal liver slices served with caramelized onions and hickory smoked bacon), and **Blackened Tenderloin** (two four-ounce tenderloin medallions, blackened with Cajun spices and served with béarnaise sauce).

History of the Landing Restaurant at Lake Alexander: Jeff and Melissa Garlie purchased the restaurant November 1, 1999. Back in the day, the restaurant was a one-room school house and, through owners, made changes turning it into a restaurant. One of the biggest changes saw it go from a bottle club to a full-service bar in February 1999. Windows were put in on the lakeside and they built around a huge oak tree so, from lakeside, guests see this huge oak coming out of the roof.

KIM'S ON PACIFIC AVENUE

119 Pacific Ave. Randall MN 56475
320-749-2994
Located one block east of Hwy 10

Most Popular Foods: Broasted Chicken and their **Homemade Soups.**
Every Sunday they have a **Brunch** buffet, serving ham, scrambled
eggs, biscuits and gravy, pancakes, broasted chicken, mashed potatoes,
and gravy, along with many other dishes.

History of Kim's on Pacific Avenue: The current owners purchased
the restaurant in October of 2006. It was originally a pizza place built
in 2001. Kim's on Pacific Avenue has a log-siding northwood's look
and feel to it with a knotty pine interior. As they have kept the pizza
business, they have also added broasted chicken and hamburgers
made of fresh hamburger from the local meat market.

A.T. The Black and White

116 1st St. SE Little Falls MN 56345
www.attheblacknwhite.com
About one mile off of Hwy 10.

Most Popular Foods: The **Black & White Express**: Dark chocolate mousse covered in dark chocolate ganache with strawberry sauce, whipped cream, and a white chocolate garnish. **Crab Omelet**: A three-egg omelet with crab, fresh spinach, and cream cheese, served with your choice of toast and hashbrowns. **Turkey Artichoke Sandwich:** Fresh ciabatta bread stuffed with turkey, a warm creamy spinach, and artichoke spread, and caramelized onions. **Signature Salad**: Lettuce, bleu cheese, Port wine poached apples, candied walnuts tossed with balsamic vinaigrette, topped with crispy fried onion straws. **Spinach & Artichoke Dip**: A warm creamy blend of cheeses, spinach and artichoke hearts, served with lightly toasted ciabatta bread.

A.T. The Black & White History: Built in 1931 as the Black and White Hamburger Shop, it was a White Castle-style diner. The Black and White has had only eight owners in its seventy-nine-year history: the Tanners, Colombes, Houles, Zettels, Sherecks, Lyschiks, and Zimmermans. Steve Colombe owned it longest, twenty-five years, from 1950 to 1975. In 1992, Ron Lyschik expanded into the vacant Jetka Hardware Store. After nearly sixteen years, Ron sold the restaurant to the current owners, Tomas and Amanda Zimmerman. It seats approximately 100 people and features a lot of the town's history and used library books. Also, one of the big attractions is the wall-length murals done by a local artist.

LOG BAR & GRILL

109 E Centre Street Royalton, MN 56373
320-584-9191
Located at the corner by the stop lights on Hwy 10

Most Popular Foods: Log Bar Burgers (half-pound burger with two cheeses, mushrooms, onions, and bacon, severed with a secret sauce on a Kaiser bun) and Homemade Pizza.

History of the Log Bar & Grill: The bar was built in 1890s. The *Royalton Banner,* attached to the bar, ran from the 1930s to 1975. The building was built by the Grahms from Little Falls. After *The Banner* closed, the space was turned into a Sandwich Shop until the 1980s. Then Eddie Derker owned the bar and took out the wall for more seating and added a kitchen.

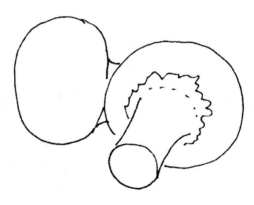

THE OLD CREAMERY CAFE

405 Main St Rice, MN. 56367
www.oldcreameryricemn.com
Located one block off Hwy 10

Most Popular Food: The Old Creamery's Grilled Sirloin Steak—hand cut sirloin steaks slow grilled and served for breakfast, lunch, or dinner.

The Old Creamery Cafe History: Built in 1914 by local farmer co-op under the name of Rice Land-O-Lakes Creamery, made butter and processed milk. They sold feed and fertilizer from 1914 to 1974. From 1974 to 1982 they only stored bulk milk and sold farm supplies, fertilizer, and feed. The Creamery was expanded four times between 1914 and the 1950s, adding can conveyer, butter room, and bulk tank bay with storage space. The Creamery moved in 1983 to a location by the side of the tracks in Rice, Minnesota, for better fertilizer and feed supplies by the railroad. In 1983 a new owner changed the use to a multi-use building with a ice cream shop, laundry, carwash, and short-order restaurant. In 1984 new owners took over and begin to make a more full-service restaurant. The present owner has been involved since 1984 and, having bought out the other owners, has changed the focus to a full-service restaurant and catering service with emphasis on country and family-style dining.

BLUE LINE SPORTS BAR & GRILL

1101 2nd Street S, Sartell, MN 56377
www.bluelinebar.com
Located three miles from Hwy 10

Most Popular Food: Burnt Ends—begin with the finest beef brisket. Secretly prepared for a slow eight-hour smoking, the meat is then cubed. Smoked again, the meat is soaked in homemade BBQ sauce. Voted Central Minnesota's best BBQ in August of 2009.

History of Blue Line Sports Bar & Grill: Scott and Esther Widor own and operate the Blue Line. While they are big fans of doing things together as a family, owning a restaurant and bar has created many "unique" togetherness opportunities. They feel they offer something more than just another sports bar and grill.

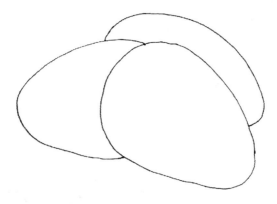

ACE BAR AND GRILL

423 E. St. Germain Street, St. Cloud, MN 56304
320-251-0232
Located three blocks from Hwy 10

Most Popular Foods: Hand-Cut Steaks (sixteen-ounce ribeye with sautéed mushrooms), **Fresh Seafood,** and their **Signature Ribs** (they make their own sauce).

History of the Ace Bar and Grill: Established in 1933 and a fixture to St Cloud's east side for many years, the restaurant was burned down twice, once in the 1960s and again in the early 1980s. It was gutted both times, but reopened each time within two years. Owners Brad and Wendy Thompson have had the business since early 2003, and they purchased it from longtime owner Jerry Larson of St. Cloud. The building is the original brick, but the interior has been renovated in the past three years and the dining room and private party room are decorated with warm colors and soft lighting.

Nix Bar & Grill

12287 Hancock St, Becker, MN 55308
They are on Facebook
On the NE corner of the intersection of Hwy 10 and Hancock Street

Most Popular Foods: Walleye Fingers, Bulldog Burger, Nix Turkey Melt, American Food—appetizers, sandwiches, salads, wraps burgers, steaks, shrimp, walleye, ribs, and pasta.

History of the Nix Bar & Grill: Nick and Shelly Mattson are the current owners since June 1, 2009. The building has been many different restaurants over the years that haven't succeeded, but they're making this a success and will be in for the long haul. They just relocated from twelve years in Ramsey, Minnesota, to Becker, Minnesota. The dining room is the original Bank of Becker from the 1800s, and they still have the vault—they use it for storage.

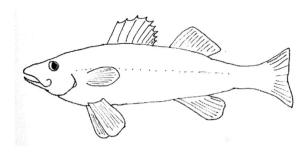

JAVA ME KRAZE

14087 Bank Street Suite #1 Becker, MN 55308
www.javamekraze.com
Located one block off Hwy 10

Most Popular Food: Java Melt—turkey, bacon, provolone, avocado, mayo, and tomato on grilled ciabatta bread.

History of the Java Me Kraze: The coffee shop has been here for approximately eight years and has gone through several changes. The new owners took over in November of 2009. They are continuing to add to and improve their menu daily. They also have a second suite available to rent daily and works great for small gatherings and business meetings.

RUSSELL'S ON THE LAKE

111 Jefferson Blvd Big Lake, MN 55309
www.russellsonthelake.com
Right on Hwy 10

Most Popular Foods: BBQ Ribs — slow-cooked tender pork ribs rubbed with their own special blend of spices. Served with Russell's own unique BBQ sauce — and their **Twenty-Ounce Prime Rib**.

History of Russell's on the Lake: A family restaurant with over twenty-five years of classic dining. Since their beginning in 1981, Russell's on the Lake's reputation for wholesome entrees and exceptional service allowed this restaurant to become a recognized destination dining location in the central Minnesota. Featuring classic dining rooms with an old world touch and amazing lake-front view, this location will continue to be home to Russell's famous entrees.

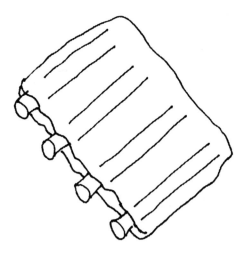

THE RICEBOX

6415 Hwy 10, Suite 112 Ramsey, MN 55303
www.thericeboxrestaurant.com
Right on Hwy 10 and Sunfish Blvd intersection

Most Popular Food Item: **Gavin Pow-Pow**, a fiery dish with a blast of flavors. Stir fry with chopped water chestnuts, celery, carrots, green peppers, onions, and peanuts in a hot & spicy sauce. The dish is served with white rice. Named after my son Gavin, which would go around tapping people with his fist saying, "Pow-Pow."

The Ricebox History: Established in 2009, the Ricebox is a family-owned restaurant with great Vietnamese food!

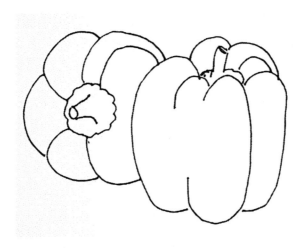

Sammy Perrella's Pizza & Restaurant

445 99th Ave NW, Coon Rapids, MN 55433
www. mysammys.com
Located one block from Hwy 10

Most Popular Food: Sammy's Special Pizza — Italian sausage, onion, and green peppe, creamy mozzarella cheese, and their zesty tomato sauce. Their Grandpa Sam's favorite pizza.

History of Sammy Perrella's Pizza & Restaurant: They've been around for a long time and become part of countless family traditions. Grandpa Sam and Grandma Louise started out with a quiet little cafe in Keewatin, Minnesota, in the early 1950s. Gramps had heard that pizza was the hottest thing in Chicago, so he went there to see what it was all about. He figured out the basics of making pizzas. When he came back, he borrowed money to buy a brick oven (the same kind they use today) and worked on recipes. Grandma told me they ate pizza every day for weeks! After a lot of trial and error, they finally perfected the legendary secret recipes still used today. They added the new pizza recipes to Grandma Louise's already fantastic menu of Italian food and rented the building at 107 East Howard Street in Hibbing, and the very first Sammy's Pizza opened on October 2, 1954. Few people remember this, but the original name was actually "La Pizzeria." Everyone called it "Sammy's Pizza," and the name stuck.

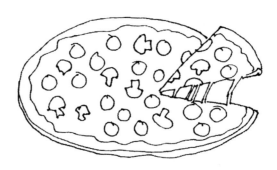

INTERSTATE 94

Interstate 94 runs from the Detroit, Michigan, westward to central Wisconsin where it merges with Interstate 90 on the journey to Billings, Montana. At Billings, I-94 ends and I-90 continues alone to Seattle, Washington. In Minnesota, I-94 runs 259 miles from the Wisconsin border through St. Paul, Minneapolis, St. Cloud, Sauk Centre, Alexandria, and Fergus Falls, on its way, to Moorhead on the border.

In the Twin Cities, I-94 crosses the picturesque Mississippi River gorge (the only length of the whole river that has a gorge), and carries some of the heaviest traffic flow in the state. I-94 serves as the main link between downtown St. Paul, the University of Minnesota main campus, and downtown Minneapolis.

The many lakes of Minnesota can be attributed to the glaciers that once covered much of the state. I-94 cuts through one of the most lake-abundant regions — Central Minnesota. Thus, the road is very busy at vacation time, carrying people to cabins and resorts.

Interesting sites along I-94 in the Twin Cities include the state Capitol and Minnesota History Center, the Science Museum, and the Children's Museum in St. Paul; in Minneapolis, the Minneapolis Institute of Arts, the Walker Art Center, and the Swedish Institute, as well as the "Chain of Lakes" of the Minneapolis Park system.

I-94 goes northwest from the Twin Cities, passing St. Cloud State University in St. Cloud, the College of St. Benedict in St. Joseph, and St. John's University in Collegeville. In Sauk Centre is the boyhood home and museum of the famous Pulitzer Prize winning author Sinclair Lewis. Nearby, the city of Alexandria houses the Kensington Runestone in their Runestone Museum.

Reference:

Barnard, R. Kent; 651-234-7504 Minnesota Department of Transportation.

The Great Minnesota Touring Book, Thomas Huhti. Trails Books, 2004.

Minnesota Department of Natural Resources http://www.dnr.state.mn.us.

SNAP DRAGON ASIAN BUFFET

625 30th Ave South, Moorhead, MN 56560
www.snapdragonasianbuffet.com
Located one-half block from I 94

Most Popular Foods: Almond Crème Wontons — slightly sweet, very addictive — and **Snap Dragon Wings** — their signature marinated chicken wings. They offer several tasty **Gluten-Free Options**. They steam the majority of their entrees. The broccoli stays crisp, the carrots tender, and the food is not laden with heavy oil. Among their most popular are **Beef Broccoli** — prepared with over twelve ingredients in the sauce alone it is full of flavor and freshness. **Thai Basil Chicken** has a tasty sauce lightly infused with fresh basil and tender white meat chicken. Their **Sweet & Sour Chicken** is like nothing you've tasted — seasoned white meat battered in a light, crunchy crust and served with a tangy sweet dipping sauce.

History of the Snap Dragon Asian Buffet: They have been preparing fresh, flavorful Asian cuisine for over sixty years. They've brought the taste of the Orient to the Midwest! Grandpa Shih began his career at the age of nine to help support the family. Later, his work ethic played an important part in his becoming a well-known chef in Szechwan (South China). The son, James Shih, apprenticed under him and, in turn, became the head chef in many restaurants in Taiwan. The son, David Shih, and his wife, Kathlene sold their thriving restaurant in Houston, Texas, to move back. With them came three generations of healthy cooking experience and a love for the Midwest.

OLE AND LENA'S PIZZERIA & MOSQUITO LANDING ICE CREAM & ANTIQUES

134 1st Avenue South West, Rothsay, MN 56579
www.oleandlenaspizzeria.com
Located downtown, less than a mile from Exit 38 on I-94

Most Popular Foods: The **Uffda Pizza, Lena's Hotdish Pizza,** the **Rothsay Reuben,** and their **Asian Chicken Salad** and desserts next door—**Homemade Waffle Cones** and **Hard Ice Cream,** candy, and antiques inside Mosquito Landing.

Ole and Lena's Pizzeria & Mosquito Landing Ice Cream & Antiques History: Opened in 2007 after an extensive renovation on Rothsay's oldest building. Packed full of history and pictures, the building will hopefully be around for another 130 years. Long before pizzas were served at Ole and Lena's Pizzeria, the town of Rothsay, Minnesota, was home to many Norwegian immigrants who probably never imagined their prized hotdish casseroles could be eaten on top of pizza. But then again, Ole and Lena has always been a couple of inventive cooks.

VIKING CAFE

203 West Lincoln Avenue Fergus Falls, MN 56537
218-736-6660
Two miles from I-94, in the heart of downtown Fergus Falls

Most Popular Foods: For breakfast: **Ham & Cheese Omelet** with toast and hashbrowns, **Bacon and Eggs** with toast and hashbrowns, and **Bisquits and Sausage Gravy** with hashbrowns. For lunch or dinner: **Hot Beef, Hot Pork,** or Hot Hamburger Sandwich with mashed potatoes and covered in homemade gravy. Daily homemade **Soups.** They make most items from scratch—pancake batter, syrup, caramel and frosted cinnamon rolls, pies, gravy, all soups, sausage gravy, baked beans, potato salad, macaroni salad, and coleslaw. They slice their own bacon from twenty-five-pound slabs and slice it so thick they only get eight slices per pound. They bone their own twenty-pound hams and slice them for breakfast meat, soups, ham dinners, and then boil the bones for soup stock. They make their own hashbrowns by boiling, cooling, peeling then shredding their own potatoes (and a lot of them!).

Viking Cafe History: In 1918 it was a general/hardware store. Around the 1930s, the Runnigan family owned a restaurant named Runnigans. The Runnigans sold to the Osterbergs. In the early 1960s the Osterbergs sold to the Hoffs, who changed the name to the Viking Cafe. In October of 1967, Lucky and Blanche Shol bought the business. They successfully ran it until December of 1998 when Lucky passed away. Blanche continued to run the business, and Blanche moved back to Fergus Falls and became a partner in 2003. In 2007, she purchased the business. To date, the cafe has existed for about eighty years, and forty-three have been with the Shol family. Lucky and Blanche had nine children, and every one worked at the cafe. Three children and three grandchildren still work here today.

GRANDMA PATTY'S CAFE

107 Central Avenue, Brandon MN 56315
320-524-2453
Located just three miles from I 94

Most Popular Food: Delight—fresh made hashbrowns or American fries mixed with bacon, sausage links, and ham, plus some mushrooms and onions and fried on the grill until golden brown, then topped with cheese. Served with eggs and toast! The best of everything breakfast!

History of Grandma Patty's Cafe: Located at 107 Central Avenue, Brandon, Minnesota, Grandma Patty's Cafe is the oldest business building still standing in town. The main part of the building was erected in 1898 and has housed a cafe of some sort ever since. Lenny and Patty Taylor are the current owners. According to their history center, they have been told that, in the past, kids shot pool at the cafe after school every day. They had a slot machine in the basement.

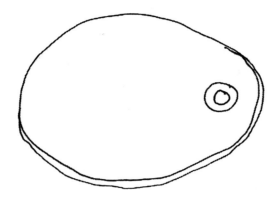

KNOTTY PINE GRILL

103 Central Avenue North Brandon, MN 56315
320-524-2814
Located 1.5 miles from I 94

Most Popular Foods: The **Knotty Pine**, features savory sautéed onions, three slices of hickory smoked bacon and is topped with creamy smokey swiss cheese all served on a lightly toasted kaiser bun. Their burgers and sandwiches are all served with "wood chips," a lightly seasoned potato chip. Other potato options are also available and they serve homemade soup seasonally. Their Broasted Chicken can't be beat! It is hot, crispy and oh, so good! Guests can order in or take it to go as they offer boxed quantities to feed the family. Made to order pizzas are also available.

History of Knotty Pine Grill: Opened in 2007 by Paul Reiland as an addition to the Knotty Pine Bait and Gas station, he also recently expanded to a second location in Elbow Lake: The Knotty Pine Bar & Grill.

Sixth Avenue Wine & Ale

115 Sixth Avenue East Alexandria, Minnesota 56308
On Facebook and Twitter
Located three miles off I 94 in downtown Alexandria

Most Popular Foods: The **Chocolate Blossom**—Belgian dark chocolate ganache with toasted walnuts wrapped in a puff pastry topped with caramel sauce and real whipped cream. The favorite appetizer is their **Wine Lover's Plate**—an assortment of meats, olives, artisan cheeses, nuts, and fruit. They offer entrées from pizzas to seafood plus a wide variety of appetizers and desserts. All their menu selections are made in-house, including pastas and ice cream. They also have fondues, both entrées and dessert. They use the freshest ingredients and locally grown produce. They serve wines, lagers, and ales.

History of Sixth Avenue Wine and Ale: The building has returned to its roots. In 1901 it was built as a saloon. Since then, it has housed everything from retail stores to a youth center. It returned to a dining establishment in July of 2006.

EDDY'S INTERLACHEN INN

4960 County Road 42 NE, Alexandria, MN 56308
www.interlacheninn.com
Located nine miles from I-94

Most Popular Foods: Pan Fried Walleye, Baked Barley, Pasta LeHommeDieu (created by the owner Gayle Backlund Haanen. Hot Italian sausage and chicken tossed with a sun-dried tomato, white wine cream sauce and served over penne noodles), **Green Olive Cheeseburgers,** and **Bloody Mary's**.

History of Eddy's Interlachen Inn: Bought from Jim Pennie (Pennie's Interlachen Inn) in December 2004 and re-opened in April 2005. The business is said to have been started in the 1940s in a small building which burned down in 1967 and the "rock" building opened in 1968. The word "Interlachen" in Scottish means "Between Two Lakes." Located between Lake's Le Homme Dieu and Lake Carlos, the name Interlachen Inn was chosen in the 1940s.

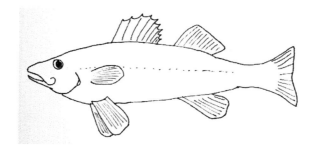

BERRIES AND MARIGOLDS BED AND BREAKFAST & EATERY

311 East 7th Street, Starbuck, MN 56381
Located about 32 miles off of Interstate 94, on Lake Minnewaska.

Most Popular Item: Sour Cream Raspberry Pie (served with whipped cream).

History of Berries and Marigolds Bed and Breakfast & Eatery: It began in 2002 as a bed and breakfast, tea room, and gift barn. It was named by the two daughters of the owners. Their grandfather used to tell the kids they were full of the berries and their grandmother used to plant marigolds everywhere, even up and down the public sidewalks. She is probably the only person who had marigolds on her casket.

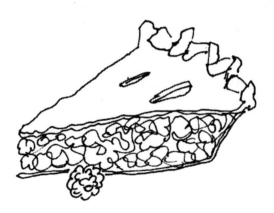

THE PALMER HOUSE HOTEL, RESTAURANT, AND PUB

500 Sinclair Lewis Avenue Sauk Centre, MN 56378
www.thepalmerhousehotel.com
Located one mile north of I-94, on State Hwy. 71, in the downtown

Most Popular Foods: Walleye (beer-battered and deep-fried to a golden brown. The sandwich is served on a toasted hoagie bun with all the condiments. The dinner entree is a larger fillet topped with sautéed onions and sliced almonds with Frangelico liqueur). Their chef's own recipe **Turtle Cheesecake** would be another.

History of the Palmer House Hotel, Restaurant, and Pub: Built in 1901 after the existing Sauk Centre House burned down, most of the building exists as it was constructed with old world craftsmanship and no power tools. The stained glass throughout the building was imported from Austria and the pub and lobby still boast the original tin ceilings. Nobel Prize winner, Sinclair Lewis worked, and lived, at the Palmer House for a period of time. The Palmer House is also a documented haunted location and has been featured in many books, articles, and is host to paranormal groups investigating on a regular basis. Many have said that it is ranked in the top five most haunted locations in the United States!

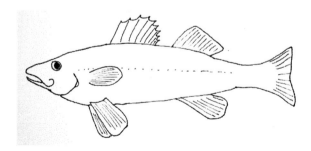

LISA'S ON MAIN

409 East Main Street, Melrose, MN 56352.
320-256-5472
Located approximately four blocks off I-94

Most Popular Foods: Homemade Soups, Sandwiches, Salads and **Wraps** daily. Their most popular wrap — **Chicken Bacon Wrap** (grilled garlic spiced chicken breast, crisp bacon, fresh organic spinach, carrots, sweet onion, tomato, parmesan cheese, and a peppercorn ranch dressing on a grilled herb wrap served with chips). The most popular lunch special — the half sandwich and choice of soup. They have specialty fair-trade coffees. They make lattes, frappes, smoothies, tea, and malts; also homemade muffins, scones, and cookies.

History of Lisa's on Main: Started June of 2000, Lisa loved going to coffee shops in New York, and thought Melrose could use one. Lisa's on Main is in the oldest existing building on Main Street in Melrose, Minnesota.

CHARLIE'S CAFE

115 Main St. East Freeport, MN 56331
www.charliescafe.com
Located two blocks off I-94

Most Popular Foods: 40-Acre Caramel Rolls (really big and covered with caramel or frosting), **Meringue Pies,** and **Roast Beef.**

History of Charlie's Cafe: Charlie Heidgerken and his brothers have been in business since 1957. Charlie started on the side street with a little four-table cafe and moved to Main Street in 1964. Charlie operated the cafe until 1999. His brother Bud ran the cafe till 2007. Jesse Job took over and still operates the cafe under Charlie's name.

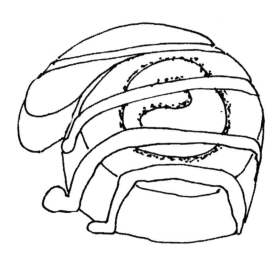

HILLCREST FAMILY RESTAURANT AND STUBBY'S TAVERN

1004 Shamrock Lane Albany MN 56307
320-845-2168
Located about three blocks off of I 94

Most Popular Food: Homemade Chicken Dumpling Soup, made fresh daily with hearty vegetables and a generous amount of dumplings. They also serve a second homemade soup daily. They have a fresh full salad bar available. Their menu consists of several club sandwiches, specialty items, homemade pizzas; breakfast served all day and much, much more.

History of HillCrest Family Restaurant and Stubby's Tavern: A locally owned, family business for over thirty years, the current owners took over the business about thirteen years ago. There is also a tavern below the restaurant that has a private entrance facing I 94. The establishment also has three private meeting rooms that can accommodate groups up to 150.

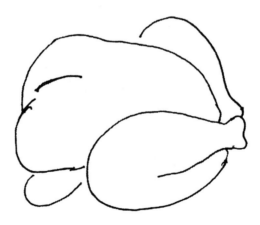

FISHER'S CLUB OF AVON

428 Stratford Road, Avon, MN 56310 (Co Rd 54 and Stratford Rd)
www.fishersclub.com
Located approximately two miles off I-94.

Most Popular Foods: Rainey Lake Walleye (walleye coated in George Fisher, Sr.'s delicate breading, deep fried and served with homemade potato salad, homemade coleslaw, and either a sweet potato or French fries), **Walleye Tacos**, and homemade **Rhubarb Pie** (homemade with ice cream on the side) and a great local beer selection (Cold Spring Brewery beers).

History of Fisher's Club of Avon: George "Showboat" Fisher retired in 1932 from ten years of major league baseball. He loved hunting and fishing, and didn't want to get tied down, so he opened Fisher's Club. The dance floor was added in 1937, and the sale of cold beer and playing of slot machines made the bar popular. He created a secret breading recipe, and the legendary Fisher's Famous Walleye began. In 1959, Junior and Sally, took over operation, expanding the kitchen. Closed during the last two years of World War II, it reopened in the summer of 1946.

Across the road from the Lake Wobegon Trail, Garrison Keillor became one of the owners in 2005. During the winter of 2006, minor updates and the addition of an outdoor lakeside deck were made. Spending hot summer nights on the lake with fine friends, good food, and a cool beverage is what Fisher's has always been about. Fishers Club is open late April through late October.

KEITH'S KETTLE FAMILY RESTAURANT

710 Nelson Drive /Hwy 24, Clearwater MN 55320
www.keithkettle.com
Loacated one-quarter mile off I-94

Most popular items: Homemade Hot Beef Sandwiches (six to eight ounces of tender sliced beef roast, bread with mashed potatoes and homemade gravy smothering it all) and **Breakfast Skillets** (fried potatoes — hash browns or American fries — beneath two fresh eggs plus selection of meats, vegetables, cheese, and sauces).

History of Keith's Kettle Family Restaurant: Built in 1980 shortly after I-94 was built through Clearwater, the original name was Prairie House (one of several around Minnesota). Keith bought the restaurant in 2001 and called it the Ole Kettle at first. He has been the operator/ owner ever since.

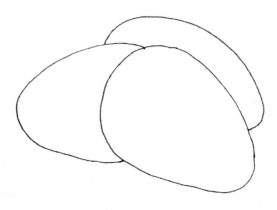

CORNERSTONE CAFE & CATERING CO.

154 West Broadway Monticello, MN 55362
www.cornerstonecafe.com
About five blocks from I-94—Hwy 25 exit north to Broadway, then left. One block down on left-hand side.

Most Popular Foods: Creamy Chicken Wild Rice Soup (made from scratch with fresh dairy cream and Minnesota wild rice) and **French Silk Pie** (made from scratch, topped with tons of real whipped cream and served in huge pieces).

Cornerstone Cafe & Catering Co. History: In the one the oldest buildings in Monticello that had housed many different shops, but it has been a cafe for over twenty-four years when purchased eight years ago. Known locally as having the best food and pie in town and enjoy a reputation for having a friendly, comfortable atmosphere and the best breakfast around, they have full bar service and can cater all occasions of any size. Everything they sell is cooked from scratch right here in their kitchen because . . . well, because it's just the way my mom raised us and they want their guests to love every bite!

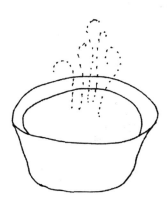

3 SQUARES RESTAURANT

12690 Arbor Lakes Parkway Maple Grove, MN 55369
www.3squaresrestaurant.com
Located 1.5 miles off I-94

Most popular item: Brie and Spinach Frittata (scrambled eggs seasoned with fresh herbs, topped with brie cheese, oven roasted tomatoes, fresh spinach, and basil chiffonade. Served with crispy hash browns and toast).

History of 3 Squares Restaurant: The Blue Plate Restaurant Company has spent over fifteen years slowly expanding and refining their definition of neighborhood restaurant, serving "sophisticated comfort food with flair." Three Squares is the Maple Grove addition to the company. Founders are David Burley and Stephanie and Luke Shimp.

David came from Western Australia with a family background in providing real hospitality in hotels and pubs. Stephanie grew up on the Mississippi River in Lake City, Minnesota, with those small town and neighborhood values that translate well at every Blue Plate restaurant. Luke joined them in 2001 after a successful career with winning NASCAR teams that taught him the value of serving the guest's needs and desires.

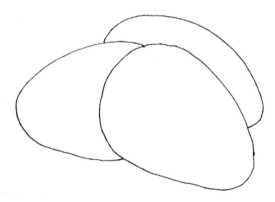

BLUE POINT RESTAURANT

739 E. Lake Street Wayzata, MN. 55391
www.bluepointrestaurantandbar.com
Located about ten miles from I-94.

Most Popular Food: Pistachio Encrusted Alaskan Halibut (pan-fried and served over bed of garnet yam puree and drizzled with toasted pumpkin seed oil. Dish of the month-*Minneapolis/St. Paul Magazine*).

Blue Point Restaurant History: Created in 1987, the concept is based upon the feel of the great seafood houses of the East Coast of the forties or fifties. The red Naugahyde booths, the hardwood flooring, the dark mahogany walls all hail from that era. The fact that the building is old (1927) lends to that authenticity. The building wasn't designed to be a restaurant but became one anyway. In fact, it has been three restaurants to date. Previous to Blue Point it was Muffaletta on the Lake, and earlier it was a classic French restaurant call La Chouette. Before its life as a restaurant the place was a gift shop, and city hall (for two years). It also was a cottage for a period of time and the oyster bar dining is rumored to have been a small store that was moved from the top of the hill behind the building.

CREMA CAFE—THE HOME OF SONNY'S ICE CREAM

3403 Lyndale Avenue South Minneapolis, MN 55408
www.cremacafeminneapolis.com
Located two miles from I 94

Most Popular Foods: Local and naturally raised Sonny Burger and homemade Veggie Burger, **Sonny's Ice Cream** and Sorbet made on premises from local organic ingredients since 1945. All the ice cream is made in small five-gallon batches and alternates between 1,000 flavors (twelve are available at any given time).

History of Crema Cafe—The Home of Sonny's Ice Cream: After World War II in 1945 at the age of twenty, Sonny worked in his uncle's ice cream shop on 34th and Nicollet, where he met Joan, called "Jiggs." Jiggs and Sonny married and purchased the uncle's business and moved it to 34th and Lyndale, adding a soda fountain. Jiggs passed away in 1980, and Sonny and son Ron closed the shop to concentrate on their wholesale business.

While Sonny and Ron made ice cream, Carrie sat in a classroom at Penn State University learning about the "technical" side of ice cream. She came home for some "hands on" training and found Sonny's Ice Cream. Ron and Carrie pooled their savings to open Crema Cafe in February of 1994 to share Sonny's Ice Cream and their passion with everyone and enjoy incredible espresso drinks, desserts, and the best homemade ice cream and sorbet.

Crema Cafe was one of the first espresso cafes in Minneapolis. After ten years, they built a kitchen where dinners and weekend breakfasts and lunches could be served. Sonny retired after the cafe opened but still made ice cream deliveries to restaurateurs he called friends. He continued to live upstairs, right on top of café, until his very last day of life on December 27, 2007. The only thing that's never changed — Sonny's Ice Cream has been made right here, cranking out one tiny batch at a time for sixty-five years.

Crema Cafe and Sonny's Ice Cream have become famous in their own Big way; calls and mail from all over the world come in daily with people inquiring about their tiny gem. Sonny's and Crema have won numerous International awards from the National Association of the Specialty Food Trade, as well as other awards from local and national associations. The Food Network has featured Sonny's and Crema Cafe on Food Finds and because of this great reputation, people come from all over the world visit Crema Cafe — the Home of Sonny's Ice Cream. They're truly grateful that people come to share their passion and plan to do what they love; serve amazing ice cream, sorbet, food and drink, and create memories of love and dedication that live on.

BE'WICHED DELI

800 Washington Avenue North., Minneapolis, MN 55401
www.bewicheddeli.com
Located approximately ½ mile southeast of the Broadway exit off I-94.

Most popular Food: Pastrami sandwich—house brined (in thyme, peppercorns, bay leaf, white wine, and salt) five days and smoked brisket from Meyer Farms of Wyoming, coated with coriander and black pepper then smoked with hickory and apple wood. They are slow roasted, sliced thinly and served with house pickled cabbage (white wine vinegar, pickling spices) and Boetjes Danish coarse-grained mustard on rye bread.

History of Be'wiched Deli: The first truly chef-driven deli in the region and dedicated to old world culinary traditions and support of sustainable, local organic agriculture when possible. The meat is without hormones or antibiotics. They cure and smoke their meats in house, then slow cook them for exquisite taste and tenderness. Their in-house pastry chef creates fresh-baked breads and desserts. The chef owners, Michael Ryan and Matthew Bickford, have spent their culinary careers in the kitchens of fine-dining restaurants, working with and learning from the industry's top talent, they honed their skills and developed relationships with farmers and foragers. Both dreamed of opening a restaurant where fresh ingredients and superior technique could be featured in a casual atmosphere. Their polished techniques and passion for quality inspired them in September 2007 to open Be'wiched Deli, a gourmet deli serving artisanal sandwiches, salads, and soups.

Supatra's Thai Cuisine

967 West 7th Street, Saint Paul, MN. 55102
www.supatra.com
Located two miles south of I-94.

Most Popular Foods: Pad Thai. Supatra's features an extensive menu of Thai dishes, including a huge selection of gluten-free items! Some other popular dishes include: **Crying Tiger** (grilled beef tenderloin), **Som Tum** (green papaya salad), **Peanut Curry Stir-fry, Crab Fried Rice, Khao Soy Noodles, Thai Catfish,** and **Fried Banana with Coconut Ice Cream.** Supatra's also offers a large selection of beers from Asia (including Singha and Chang from Thailand), along with a variety of locally produced beers.

History of Supatra's Thai Cuisine: Established in 2004 and moved to the present location on West Seventh Street in 2007. Before she opened the restaurant, Supatra published a cookbook, *Crying Tiger: Thai Recipes from the Heart.* She offers Thai cooking classes at the restaurant, featuring some of her most popular dishes.

Great Waters Brewing Company

426 Saint Peter Street, St. Paul, MN 55102
www.greatwatersbc.com
Located just four blocks from I 94

Most Popular Foods: Known for their fabulous **Beer** selection including four-cask conditioned ales. Their menu features great salads and tasty sandwiches, including their **Great Waters' Reuben**, a pastrami and turkey combo on marbled rye. They have many vegetarian options, and their children's menu includes home made root beer.

History of Great Waters Brewing Company: Opened in 1997 in the Historic Hamm Building built in 1913, they are in the heart of downtown St. Paul. Their award-winning beers are brewed on premise using well water and premium ingredients from around the world. Great Waters has up to ten of their own beers on tap including four-cask conditioned ales, known for their flavor and mouth feel.

THE BUNGALOW RESTAURANT & BAR

1151 Rivercrest Road Lakeland, MN 55043
www.bungalowinn.net
About one block north of I94 on the river side of the St.Croix trail.

Most Popular Foods: **Steaks** and **Seafood**, and the **Lake Perch Basket** (generous portion of crispy fried yellow lake perch in a basket of seasoned fries with coleslaw, pumpernickel bread, and homemade tartar sauce).

History of the Bungalow Restaurant & Bar: The Bungalow began in 1931. Highway 12 (now I-94) passed right by their front door, and the toll bridge to Hudson, Wisconsin, was up the road. Original owners, Milbert and Lilly Clymer, sold Phillips 66 gas and food for weary travelers at what was then called "the Station." They kept the place open around the clock; sleeping attendants woke to serve the bell-ringing late-hour patrons. With prohibition in effect, bootleg whiskey and slot machines offered fun time for those who knew Milbert and Lilly well enough. A hidden room housed the moonshine and slot machines, as they never knew when they might get raided. During the gangster era of the early 1930s, Milbert and Lilly saw Babyface Nelson, Alvin Karpis, Ma Barker and her boys, and even John Dillinger. St.Paul was a haven for bad guys then.

In 1969, Jack and Jan Lifteau bought the property, adding a kitchen and dining room and renaming it the Bungalow Inn. A Dixieland jazz ensemble, the Mouldy Figs, played on Sundays, Jack bartended, and Jan was the chief cook. They ran the tavern for thirty-one years, and the Bungalow flourished. Now under Bill Eisenmann, a kitchen-man from Chicago, his wife Karen, and close friends, the Bungalow is a roadhouse destination for hungry travelers and area residents alike. The crowd still gambles, the booze still flows, and the steaks, chops, and walleye dinners are better than ever.

INTERSTATE 90

Interstate Highway 90 — a transcontinental link between Boston and Seattle — crosses the southernmost portion of Minnesota. Just above the Iowa border, en route from Wisconsin, to South Dakota, Highway 90 passes through or near the Minnesota cities of Rochester, Austin, Albert Lea, Fairmont, and Worthington.

Along its route, the highway spans a great variety of geological formations, from the hills, valleys, forests, and bluffs of the "driftless area" of southeastern Minnesota — unmarred by ancient glaciers — to the flat, drier prairies of the west. In fact, though Minnesota has an abundance of lakes — more than 13,000 totals — the four counties that do not have any natural lakes (Rock, Pipestone, Mower, and Olmsted) are all on or near I-90.

Two intriguing state parks near the highway in the far west are Pipestone and Blue Mounds. Pipestone is known for the reddish, soft rock that Native Americans have used for centuries for carvings of ceremonial pipes. Blue Mounds State Park is home to a herd of bison as well as virgin prairie.

In the middle of the state, I-90 passes through Austin, home of Hormel Foods and the famous Spam Museum. Nearby is Mystery Cave State Park, which has more than thirteen miles of underground passages.

The eastern most portion of I-90 travels through the Richard Dorer Memorial Hardwood Forest. The park has eight campgrounds, and features hiking, bird watching, horseback riding, mountain biking, and motorized trail riding.

References:

Barnard, R. Kent; 651-234-7504 Minnesota Department of Transportation

The Great Minnesota Touring Book, Thomas Huhti. Trails Books, 2004.

Minnesota Department of Natural Resources http://www.dnr.state.mn.us

CHIT CHAT'S FAMILY RESTAURANT

920 S Kniss Ave, Luverne, MN 56156
507-283-4458
Located one and a half blocks north of I 90

Most Popular Food: Breakfast Omelets. They use only USDA Grade AA eggs and whip them with just the right amount of milk to give them that little extra fluff. They use real shredded cheddar cheese and top the omelet with whatever the customer wants. Whether it's a **Ham and Cheese** or a **Build Your Own** with bacon, ham, sausage, peppers, onions, mushrooms, tomatoes, salsa, and even jalapenos. Omelets are served with hash browns and toast.

History of Chit Chat's Family Restaurant: Founded in 1996 by current owners Don and Crystal Ellefson, the restaurant was formerly a Country Kitchen originally opened in 1978. In 1995, after several years in the foodservice industry, Don wanted to go into business on his own. After hurdles and obstacles, Chit Chits opened in the spring of 1996. Although the basic business hasn't changed that much, they do things with a more hands-on approach, taking their cooking to "like grandma used to make."

MAGNOLIA RESTAURANT AND BAR

1202 South Kniss Avenue Luverne, MN 56156
507-283-9161
Located directly off the exit of I-90 & S Highway 75,
next to the Super 8 Motel

Most Popular Foods: Homemade Onion Rings and **Aged Steaks** (custom-aged in house to ensure tenderness and flavor, each piece of meat is hand cut daily by their on-premise meat cutter, Vern Vis. Their steaks are broiled to customer liking and seasoned with Mag Seasoning blend). Their hamburger is ground on site daily and is very lean.

History of Magnolia Restaurant and Bar: In 1938 A.C. Dispanet opened the Magnolia Bar and Steak House, which soon became known throughout the upper Midwest for its food, drink, and congenial atmosphere. The restaurant suffered an unfortunate fire and had to be relocated a couple of times before finally settling in Luverne, Minnesota. They continue to boast a fully stocked bar, as well as on-premise custom-aged hand-cut steaks, seafood, and specialty dishes.

BenLee's Cafe

212 10th Street, Worthington, MN 56187
www.benleescafe.com   507-343-3400
Located downtown Worthington, approximately ten blocks off I-90

Most Popular Foods: The Gyan Panini (grilled chicken, four cheeses, smoked bacon, pecans, and craisens grilled on their Panini grill on a croissant) and the **Apple Walnut Craisen Salad** (apples, walnuts, and craisens, plus grilled chicken and a homemade poppy seed dressing).

History of BenLee's Cafe: Opened in 2005, the name is a combination of their sons's names, Ben and Lee. Ben and his wife live in North Carolina along with his two sons, and Lee passed away in June of 2005 at age seventeen. He loved coffee shops. The business moved to Worthington in 2008. BenLee's is known for perhaps a healthier menu, with no fried foods, but wraps, panini, salads, homemade soups, and sandwiches. Of course there are always some homemade treats on the counter to enjoy with coffee or lattes. Smoothies and Frappes are also available.

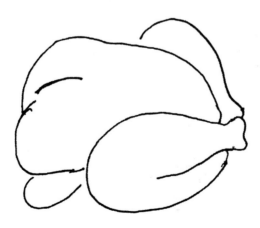

PILLAR'S PUB & EATERY

507 2nd St. Jackson, MN 56143
507-847-9901
Located 1.5 miles south of I-90

Most Popular Food: Pillar's Penne Pasta with Pesto, tossed with feta cheese, peppers, onions, and Italian sausage. Served with a side salad and garlic breadstick.

History of Pillar's Pub & Eatery: Opened September 22, 2008, in a converted an old bank building, it has the historical high ceilings with a lot of decor. They tried to leave as much of the history as they could, even using the marble from the teller's stations as the bar. As a family-owned restaurant, all members work there. Troy (owner) manages the day-to-day operations. Wife, Jadee, does the bookwork and waitresses. Son Taylor is a waiter, son Tanner cooks, and daughter Tiara washes and helps out where she can. She can't wait to be a waitress for her dad. Troy opened the restaurant because he wanted the freedom to enjoy his kids growing up.

CUP N SAUCER CAFE & SWEET SHOPPE

23 N. Main St. Sherburn, MN. 56171
507-764-6721
Located three-quarters of a mile south of I-90 on Hwy 4

Most Popular Food: Potato Salad (sixty-five-year-old Family recipe)

History of Cup N Saucer Cafe & Sweet Shoppe. Opened in June of 1953 by Patricia and Woody Hanson. In the 1960s and early 1970s a lot of time spent by school kids as a (drive-in) after games. They offered adult coffee time to visit and ice shaking. The 1970s brought catering into the picture and kept the family busy and active. Also they served Sunday Smorgasbords and Lutefisk & Lefsa buffets. Through the 1990s both dining rooms were remodeled. In 1981 Woody passed away so it left Mom alone running and managing it along with Dan, Dave, Tim, and Terri and the third generation to carry on the tradition. As of 2006, Mom was laid up with hip problems so Dan and Terri took over the business and enjoy serving the community and travelers that stop by.

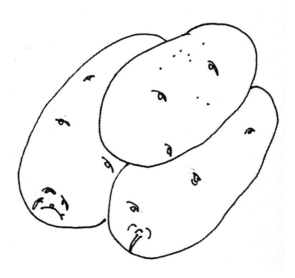

KORTE'S BAR & GRILL

319 South Dugan Welcome MN. 56181
507-728-8820
Located two miles south from Welcome exit of I-90.

Most Popular Food: Beef Commercial — beef sandwich with potatoes with lots of beef gravy.

History of Korte's Bar & Grill: Korte's Bar & Grill has been operating for two years by Diane Korte.

THE RANCH FAMILY RESTAURANT

1330 North State Street Fairmont, MN 56031
www.theranchrestaruant.com
Located ½ mile south of I-90 on Hwy 15

Most Popular Foods: Huge Salad Bar (with a combination of fresh fruits, vegetables, salads, and two home cooked soups) with over forty items. **Specialty Sandwiches, Steaks,** and **Seafood** with a cocktail lounge.

History of the Ranch Family Restaurant: Family owned and operated by Steve and JoAnn Schmitz with their son Kevin since June 4, 1981.

EL AGAVE MEXICAN RESTARAUNT

62 Downtown Plaza Fairmont, MN 56031
507-235-8835
Located downtown Fairmont about three miles from I-90

Most Popular Foods: Burrito Cancun, Tamales, Tostadas, Quesadillas, Chalupas, Enchiladas. They have all kinds of combinations and use special sauces and mixed condiments to give the flavor of Mexico.

History of El Agave Mexican Restaurant: Having been in Fairmont for nine years, in 2007 they sold the restaurant, changing the ownership name and adding a few new items.

CRESCENDO EXQUISITE FOOD AND FINE WINES

118 S. Broadway Ave (Downtown) Albert Lea, MN 56007
www.crescendodining.com
Located in downtown Albert Lea, about three miles from I-90

Most Popular Foods: Their **Filet Mignon** (dry aged, prime, the finest available, is served to order and topped with a made-on-the-spot brandy and shallot reduction and accompanied with their parmesan mashed potatoes and sautéed asparagus) is their mainstay, **Fresh Seafood** (varies according to the menu and is served with seasonally relevant sides and is always a visual as well as tasty work of art) is also popular.

Crescendo Exquisite Food and Fine Wines History: Crescendo opened in May of 2001. It features a regularly changing menu (every six weeks or so) and foods in the "California Gourmet" style. This style borrows influences of classic French and Italian origin, with occasional Eastern departures: always an emphasis upon locally raised produce and livestock if possible. Each dish is as visually pleasing as deliciously satisfying. A baby grand piano is situated in the  dining room, in a remodeled building dating from 1886. Chef Robert Tewes plays the piano live each evening when he isn't needed in the kitchen. A meal at Crescendo is a memorable event. They have received many awards including favorable reviews by both the *Star Tribune* and *Minnesota Monthly*.

Lakeside Café & Creamery

408 Bridge Avenue, Albert Lea, MN 56007
Three miles south of I-90, Exit 157 (County 22/Bridge Avenue), on
the left opposite the lake

Most Popular foods: In the morning it's the **Coffee** (great brewed coffee and espresso drinks paired with home-baked cinnamon or caramel rolls, cinnamon twists and scones) and **French Toast**. Noon and evenings it's the Combo Specials (deli-style sandwiches, some grilled as Paninis, on a choice of six breads baked right here. Half sandwiches are actually three-quarter sandwiches, so people team them up with a cup of soup, of which there are three choices plus chili every day and served with a dill pickle spear and choice of kettle chips or a fresh fruit kabob). All day it's the **Fresh Fruit Smoothies** (five flavors).

History of the Lakeside Cafe and Creamery: Albert Lea's original Lakeside Café opened in 1947 at the corner of Wilson Street and Bridge Avenue, where they are today. Seating just twenty-five people, Thomas and Julia Sonksen inspired a loyal and devoted following with their home-cooked meals and home-baked pies and pastries. Sold in 1974 to Clifford and Izola Haried and in 1983 to Barb Swenson the Lakeside Café served generations of Albert Lea residents until its closing in 1988. Reborn in 1999, The Lakeside Café & Creamery continues the fine traditions of quality and value, satisfying today's desire for home cooked goodness, ice cream treats, and gourmet coffee drinks.

CASA ZAMORA

2006 East Main Street Albert Lea Minnesota 56007
Located three miles from I-90.

Most Popular Food: The **Enchilada** — not the typical red sauce, green sauce, chocolate, or cheese they specialize in authentic enchilada gravy. Their most popular enchilada consists of a flour tortilla stuffed with ground beef then layered with their signature enchilada gravy and topped with freshly grated cheese before baking in an oven and served on a hot plate table side. However, they have several different flavor profiles to choose from besides interchanging flour and corn tortillas they also offer chicken, sour cream, cheese, bean, queso, seafood, shrimp, and shredded beef enchiladas.

Casa Zamora History: Originating in 1969, Casa Zamora a family-owned and operated authentic Mexican restaurant in Albert Lea, Minnesota. Their history began centuries ago as entire Mexican civilizations were built and centered on family and food. Staying true to its roots, the Zamora family still works together and has more than a century and a half of combined in-house experience and more than four decades of restaurant service. For the past three consecutive years they won the Readers Choices Award and were voted "Best Mexican Food" by the readers of the *Albert Lea Tribune*.

KORNER KAFE

101 W Front St. Hayward, MN 56043
507-373-0513
Located about one mile south of I-90 on Hwy 26 and two blocks east
on the first turn after the train tracks on Front Street.

Most Popular Food: Homemade French Fries. They cut and fry their
own french fries. They are known for home cooking. They serve a daily
special plus have a large menu featuring the best burgers served in the
area.

History of the Korner Kafe: The cafe is the feature of the town and
has been around for over twenty-five years. It is and has been the
gathering place for town residents every day and features the coffee
club of about twenty residents who gather daily for friendly chatter.
Non members are always welcomed and treated as special guests.

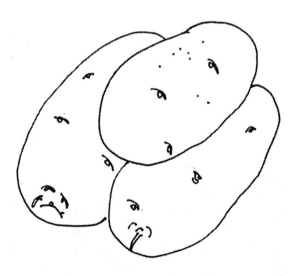

THE OLD MILL RESTAURANT

54446 24th Street, Austin, MN 55912
www.oldmill.net
Located two miles north of I-90.

Most Popular Food: Beef — hand-cut prime steaks. Their prime rib is the good old-fashioned standing rib roast unlike most others who serve a ribeye.

History of the Old Mill Restaurant: Opened in 1950 in a flour mill built in 1864. Diners have a view overlooking the Ramsey Dam and Cedar River. Dave Forland has owned and operated the restaurant since 1988.

PIGGY BLUES BBQ

323 N. Main Street, Austin, MN, 55912
www.PiggyBluesBBQ.com
Located approximately one mile south of I-90
(6th St. NE exit) or (Hormel exit).

Most Popular Foods: Shredded Pork Sandwich with **Pit Potatoes**. Specially seasoned pork shoulder, slow cooked for twelve hours. It is then shredded and served on a fresh baked French roll accompanied with fresh potato slices that are deep-fried until golden. Their food is not sauced. They serve a variety of homemade sauces on the side.

Piggy Blues BBQ History: Started when Ronald Meyer decided there was a need for good "Q" in Austin, and armed with decades of meat knowledge and practice smoking meats in the backyard, not to mention countless experiences eating at BBQ joints around the country, Piggy Blues BBQ was born. Ron couldn't do it alone, so he recruited his son-in-law, BBQ fanatic Josh Diaz as his business partner. Over the past ten years Ron, Josh, family, and loyal employees have made a successful team. Through the years, Piggy Blues has expanded into mobile concessions and a busy catering business. Winning many local and regional awards for not only outstanding smoked ribs, beef brisket, and pork, but also for their burgers, side dishes, and Po' Boy sandwiches.

OASIS BAR AND GRILL

123 main Street Dexter Minnesota 55926
507-584-9914
Only one-half mile from I-90 in downtown Dexter

Most Popular Food: Their most popular is the six-ounce **Ribeye Sandwich**. They also serve shrimp, chicken fish, world famous hamburgers, and homemade pizza

History of the Oasis Bar and Grill: In business since May 1, 2000, the restaurant has been in business since the 1930s. Johnny Cash stopped in the early sixties. Jan and Terry are the hosts.

Sammy's Family Restaurant

115 South Main Street, Stewartville, MN 55976
www. sammyscatering.com
Located two miles south of I-90 on Hwy 63

Most Popular Food: Chicken Salad Plate—made it from scratch it's different from most chicken salads because it has grapes in it. This sounds a little weird I know but when you mix the sweetness of the grapes with the saltiness of the shoestring potatoes it is served on, the plate really comes together.

History of Sammy's Family Restaurant: Started by his dad, Terry, and him in November of 1999. After two weeks getting slammed in the kitchen, dad couldn't take it anymore so brother Seth came on board. Ten years later, Seth and he own and operate Sammy's with their wives, Missy and Tayla, respectively.

CABIN COFFEE COMPANY

466 West 6th Street St. Charles, MN 55972
www.cabincoffeeco.com
Located one mile off I-90 on Hwy 14

Most Popular Food: Fresh Roasted Coffee, Egg Sandwiches, Tomato Bisque Soup, Smoked Chicken Salad. Their breakfast menu offers Egg Sandwiches, Scones, Cinnamon Rolls, Muffins, Fresh baked Bagels, and Coffee Cakes. Their lunch menu offers Soups, Deli Sandwiches, Smoked Chicken Salad, BBQ Pork Sandwiches, and Chef Salad. Their beverage menu includes Lattes, Mochas, Frappes, Italian Sodas, Smoothies, Fresh Brewed Iced tea, and Coke Products.

Cabin Coffee Company History: A franchise originated in Clear Lake, Iowa, they were there first franchise store. They have been open since November 2007. The Iowa location has a total of four stores with more starting soon. They are the only Minnesota store. Their atmosphere is very cozy — with a fireplace, western décor, saddle to sit on and their very own roasting house. They roast beans fresh every day. Their customers can dine in or come through their drive thru.

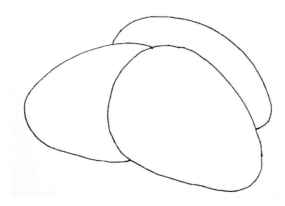

Amish Market Square

2850 Whitewater Ave., St. Charles, MN 55972
507-932-5908
Located three blocks south of I-90, Exit 233

Most Popular Foods: Chicken Dinner. They offer a home-style menu featuring their homemade goods and recipes. They also make their own jams, jellies, and preserves, which are also offered for many of their breakfast meals. The fruits are from the Amish children who pick organic berries. Most of the vegetables that they serve and that are used in their homemade soups are grown on local Amish farms.

History of the Amish Market Square: Their restaurant is quiet and offers free WI-FI for those who need a break from traveling. Their booths and tables are made of oak by the local Amish communities. Servers wear Amish-made aprons and offer a wide variety of beverages. If guests choose to dine off the menu, they will find a large selection. An early diner can enjoy the unique apple crunch bread French toast or their Amos's omelet served with their very own wheat berry bread. They stock their convenience store with fresh restaurant foods and soups for a quick meal. Their bakery products are very popular with "on the go" travelers.

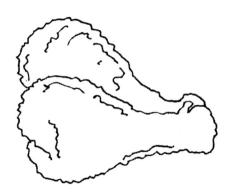

BLUE HERON COFFEEHOUSE

162 W. 2nd St., Winona, MN 55987
507-452-7020
Located seven miles from I-90

Most Popular Foods: Their menu includes coffee, espresso, tea, beverages, soups, salads, sandwiches, pastries and desserts, many of them vegetarian, vegan, and gluten free. All the food at Blue Heron Coffeehouse is made in-house, from scratch, using organically grown and locally produced ingredients whenever possible.

History of Blue Heron Coffeehouse: Begun in September 1998, directly across from Winona State University. In 2006 they relocated to downtown Winona, which is larger and attached to the Bookshelf, an independent bookseller.

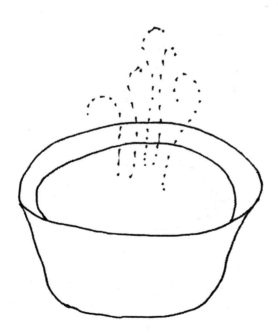

CORKY'S PIZZA AND ICE CREAM

25 South Walnut Street, La Crescent, MN 55947
507-895-6996
Located about one mile off I-90

Most Popular Food: Pizza. For twenty-five years, they have made Southeastern Minnesota's finest pizza. They make their own pizza dough each day and create their own pizza sauce from scratch. They grind their own Italian sausage, as well as blend a mix of mozzarella and provolone cheeses. They offer a very thin crust pizza or a Chicago pan style pizza. Corky's Special Pizza is topped with sausage, mushrooms, olives, onions, and green peppers, and cheese. Their Taco Pizza is unique and delicious. A special sauce is used. It is topped with shredded lettuce, crushed nacho chips, tomatoes, and cheddar cheese. They offer sour cream and taco sauce on the side.

History of Corky's Pizza: It was founded in 1985, by Alger "Corky" Shillings in La Crescent, Minnesota. The first menu consisted of pizza, ice cream, and a few sandwiches. Corky retired in 1987 and sold the business to Troy and Suzanne Nolop. The menu has been expanded over the years to include cheeseburgers, sandwiches, soups, and salads, as well as many ice cream desserts and apple pie, in addition to pizza. In 1989 Corky's Video was added to the business in the neighboring space. Troy and Suzanne have three children who like to help out at the restaurant and help to create a family atmosphere.

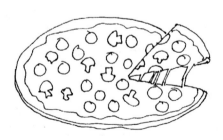